ᵀᴴᴱONCE-A-WEEK
GARDENER

THE ONCE-A-WEEK GARDENER

Time-saving tips and essential tasks season-by-season

CAROLYN HUTCHINSON

CHANCELLOR PRESS

First published in 1999
by Mitchell Beazley, an imprint of
Octopus Publishing Group Ltd,
2-4Heron Quays,
London E14 4JP
Reprinted in 1999, 2001

This edition published in 2003
by Chancellor Press, an imprint of
Bounty Books, a division of
Octopus Publishing Group Ltd,
2-4 Heron Quays,
London E14 4JP

Reprinted 2004

ISBN 0 7537 0740 3

A CIP catalogue copy of this
book is available from the British Library

Executive Editor: Alison Starling
Executive Art Editor: Vivienne Brar
Senior Editor: Michèle Byam
Designers: Graham Jenks
and Helen Taylor
Production: Rachel Staveley
Picture Research: Jenny Faithfull
Illustrator: Ian Sidaway
Indexer: Ann Barrett

Set in Giovanni Book

Printed and bound in China by
Toppan Printing Company Limited

Contents

Introduction

Once-a-week gardening can be quick and easy work, and produce wonderful results.

Gardening can be both immensely pleasurable and rewarding, but for busy people – with demanding jobs or young families, perhaps – keeping the garden in shape can seem an awesome chore. However, this need not be the case. Whatever your aims – whether you enjoy gardening for its own sake, or just want to create an agreeable space for relaxing and entertaining – with the help of this book, you will find that gardening is much easier, and a good deal less time-consuming, than you think.

All the projects in the book are basic and apply to gardens of all sizes, shapes and styles. They are arranged by season, so that you can tell at a glance what you should be doing at any particular time of the year.

The number of tasks in a specific season may seem daunting, but do not feel you have to undertake them all at once. The grading system of exclamation marks at the start of each project indicates how important it is: you should simply check the gradings as each season begins, and prioritize the tasks to suit you and your garden. For the absolutely essential jobs, there is always an explanation as to why they are so vital – the once-a-week gardener, pushed for time, deserves a justification for the effort expended on any particular task.

Approximate timings for each project are given so that you can plan your time, and encourage you to get started. Most gardening work is intimidating in prospect, but it is surprising how much can be achieved quite quickly.

Many of the step-by-step projects exhibit extremely useful time-saving tips and techniques. However, some tasks are inevitably painstaking, and cannot be hurried. Remember that by doing things thoroughly in the first place, you will usually save a lot of time in the long term – preparing the ground for turfing, for instance, is heavy work, but it is an insurance against future problems that may well take hours to put right later. Similarly, following the correct planting method guarantees the best start for your plants, while a rushed

session can lead to an inordinate amount of trouble as you try to revive struggling, sickly specimens.

The plant directory at the back of the book contains those plants that will grow beautifully with minimal effort. If you follow the siting and soil recommendations given, this will give your plants a huge headstart, again saving you time, trouble and expense later. A sun-loving plant such as ceanothus, for instance, will be miserable in a shady position, but other equally lovely shrubs, such as philadelphus and mahonia, will thrive. Similarly, an attempt to grow rhododendrons in anything but acid soil is a thankless task. Working *with* your soil type, rather than against it, and setting plants in the right position, really does make all the difference.

There is no real mystery to gardening – each task is simply a series of steps. If you follow the steps through, you will be amazed by how much easier the garden is to look after in the long run. The plants will be happier and healthier, and they will do the growing for you – just what is needed for those gardeners with busy lives.

SEASONAL TASKS

This chart provides an at-a-glance guide to all the step-by-step seasonal tasks outlined on pp. 14–123, including seasonal reminders of those tasks that can be undertaken at different times of the year; laying turf, for instance, is probably best done in mid-spring, but can also be carried out in autumn.

You do not have to complete a task within a particular season – if you live in a colder part of the country, for instance, you may have to delay tasks such as spring planting or sowing, while if you live in a warmer region you may be able to undertake them earlier than advised in this book.

EARLY SPRING

- Plant hardy perennials, wall shrubs and climbers (which can also be done in autumn), and small alpines in walls and crevices
- Renew rock garden top-dressing
- Feed and mulch border plants
- Prune shrubs that flower on this year's new stems such as summer-flowering spiraea; roses (large-flowered, cluster-flowered, patio, miniature, groundcover); dogwoods (*Cornus*); eucalyptus; honeysuckle (*Lonicera*); evergreen climbers (as for deciduous climbers in winter)

MID-SPRING

- Stake taller herbaceous perennials in the early stages
- Dead-head and feed bulbs after flowering, and remove unsightly foliage as it dies back
- Begin regular hedge trimming
- Renovate overgrown evergreen hedges now, deciduous hedges in late winter
- Prune evergreen shrubs and conifers to shape them up
- Feed all container-grown trees

LATE SPRING

- Prune deciduous spring shrubs, such as flowering currant (*Ribes*), forsythia and kerria after flowering
- Select bedding plants carefully, checking for vigour, a good root system and no sign of stress, dryness or pests and diseases
- Plant out bedding plants in any reasonable soil for summer displays
- Plant up the pond with marginal plants, oxygenators such as elodea and waterlilies (*Nymphaea*)

EARLY SUMMER

- Regularly remove spent rose flowers to promote further blooms
- Prune early large-flowered clematis, such as 'Nelly Moser' or 'The President' to encourage a smaller flush of flower in autumn
- Prune early species clematis such as *Clematis armandii* and *C. alpina*
- Conserve water by using water butts and seep hose, and by carefully

MIDSUMMER

- Cut back faded flowers of hardy perennials to promote a second flush
- Feed repeat- or continuous-flowering roses after the first flush
- Use mulches or plant pot 'reservoirs' to keep vulnerable plants moist
- Provide support for climbers and train in regularly
- Prune back summer shrubs, such as deutzia, that flower on the previous year's stems (as for *Ribes* in late spring)

Beds, borders and pools   Kitchen gardens   ◖ Approximate timing of task

 Propagation   Pests and diseases   ■ Task can be undertaken in other season(s)

 Containers   Priority of task

 Lawns   **!!!** high   **!!** medium   **!** low

• Sow border annuals *in situ*
• Divide perennials (can also be done in late autumn)
Propagate a wide range of shrubs and climbers by layering
• Take basal stem cuttings from hardy perennials

Repot overwintered container plants such as geraniums
• Spring-clean paved areas
• Sow seed of tender bedding plants and vegetables indoors
Rake and aerate the lawn by spiking, and apply a top-dressing

to improve soil condition
Make the first sowings of hardy vegetables in the garden

---

and shrubs, repot and top-dress if necessary and top-dress mature plants
Begin the regular routine of lawn mowing and trimming the edges
• Prepare the ground for turfing and sowing if required

• Create new lawns from turf or sow seed now or in mid-autumn
• Overseed worn, patchy areas of grass, level any lumps or hollows, and repair worn edges, now or in autumn
Make the first sowings and

plantings in a raised vegetable bed
• Plant no-dig early potatoes, loose-leaf lettuce and carrots
• Protect tender young crops from late frosts
• Plant container-grown herbs in pots

Propagate pond plants including iris and waterlilies
• Take softwood cuttings of a wide range of shrubs and climbers
Plant up pots, tubs and window boxes for colourful summer displays

of bedding plants
• Plant up hanging baskets, flower towers and pouches
Feed the lawn, using granular or liquid fertilizer. It may need feeding again in mid-autumn

• Continue to mow the lawn and trim the edges

---

directed hand-watering
Divide up congested clumps of spring bulbs when the leaves are beginning to die back
Keep container plantings looking

good by regular dead-heading, watering and mulching
Plant up tomatoes and other fruit and vegetables in growbags for late summer and autumn crops

Mow the lawn on a regular basis, and keep edges trimmed

• Tidy the pond and thin out overcrowded oxygenators
• Remove suckers from grafted plants, and from the base of trees
Take semi-ripe cuttings of shrubs and climbers

• Root cuttings in water
Install a patio watering system if hand-watering is becoming a chore
• Feed permanent container plants (as in mid-spring)
Water lawn thoroughly, raise

mower blades and remove grass box to protect lawn from drought
Protect crops from pests
• Prune apple and pear trees
• Harvest, then dry or freeze herbs

SEASONAL TASKS

LATE SUMMER

☞ Summer prune wisteria and train in new plants (the second stage of pruning and training wisteria is in late winter)
• Prune rambling roses after flowering, and tie in new growths

• Repair fences and other wooden structures and paint fences and garden sheds with preservative
• Remove crumbling mortar from walls and repoint
🪣 Prepare containers for holiday

EARLY AUTUMN

☞ Tidy borders by cutting back faded flowers, removing litter and any redundant plant supports, and lightly forking any bare soil
• Plant container-grown trees and shrubs between now and late autumn
• Plant out spring bulbs over the

next few weeks, delaying tulip planting until mid- to late autumn
🪣 Plant up spring bulbs in pots and tubs, delaying tulip planting until mid-to late autumn
• Bring tender perennials, such as geraniums, indoors, pot up, trim

MID-AUTUMN

☞ Prune back taller shrubs, such as roses and lavatera, to prevent root damage caused by wind-rock
• Transplant evergreen shrubs and conifers as necessary
• Plant clematis to climb through trees, setting them deeper than they were in the original pot

• Plant hardy wall shrubs, climbers and hardy perennials up to late autumn if not done in early spring
• Prune climbing roses after flowering and tie in new growth
• Clear up the rock garden by removing fallen leaves, faded flowers and dead top-growth

LATE AUTUMN

☞ Take measures to protect plants and garden structures from the damage caused by winter winds
• Plant bare-root trees and stake them securely
• Plant bare-root roses
• Transplant deciduous shrubs when dormant between now and early spring (use the same method as for

evergreen shrubs in mid-autumn)
• Clear up the garden by removing all faded top-growth of herbaceous plants and any litter or debris, and by sweeping paths and patios
• Feed the birds and provide nest-boxes to encourage them to use the garden as a base from which to search out overwintering pests

WINTER

☞ Shape up deciduous climbers in early winter, removing congested and unwanted growth
• Plant hedging plants in early winter, preparing the ground thoroughly
• Hard prune late-flowering clematis such as 'Perle d'Azur' in late winter

• Carry out the second stage of wisteria pruning and training in late winter
• Train newly planted hedges to encourage densely bushy growth
• In late winter, renovate deciduous hedges in the same way as for evergreen hedges in mid-spring

absences by dead-heading, treating pests and standing them in a shady spot or setting up a home-made watering system

🍑 Maximize crops by feeding, mulching and regular picking

• Plant out strawberries for good crops next year

🔺 Continue mowing and keeping the lawn edges trim

• Use the same measures as in midsummer (thorough watering,

mowing higher than normal, etc.), if there is a prolonged drought

---

back and overwinter

🔺 Create lawns from seed in well-prepared ground

• Overseed worn patches and level humps and hollows at any time through autumn, if not already done in mid-spring

• Continue to mow and edge the lawn as necessary until growth ceases later in the autumn or winter

🍑 Pot up garden herbs, such as mint and chives, and bring indoors for winter use

• Plant out spring cabbages in any

vacant ground, preferably in an open, sunny site

• Cut back dead or dying top-growth of pond plants and remove fallen leaves regularly, or net the whole pond to prevent pollution

• Collect and save ripe seed

• Recycle waste plant material by composting, shredding or digging in to improve the soil

• Make your own compost from garden and kitchen waste, using wooden or plastic bins

🌱 Propagate shrubs by layering between now and late autumn if not done in early spring

🪴 Plant up containers with colourful winter bedding plants

🔺 Repair damaged lawn edges

• Renovate lawns by spiking, etc., if not already done in early spring

• Create lawns from turf or seed between now and late autumn, if not already done in mid-spring

• Feed the lawn, in the same way as in late spring, if it is looking jaded

---

• Assess the overall structure of the garden and plan for simple changes such as altering the shape of the lawn

• Collect fallen leaves and compost them in a leaf cage or in plastic sacks

• Prepare new ground for border plantings and kitchen beds by digging thoroughly and then

incorporating organic matter

• Protect garden plants from frost and snow with cloches and fleece, and install a heater if there are fish in the pond to ensure an ice-free area

🌱 Divide overcrowded clumps of hardy perennials such as red hot pokers (*Kniphofia*)

• Take hardwood cuttings of trees,

shrubs and climbers

🪴 Pot up lily bulbs for summer colour and scent

• Protect containers and container plantings against frost

🍑 Create a raised vegetable bed

• Prune out any unbalanced or upright unwanted growth on weeping standard trees

• Undertake the removal of tree branches as necessary, ensuring a clean cut

• Continue dividing hardy perennials during mild spells, in the same way

as in late autumn

• Clean out all pots and trays, clean and oil lawn mowers, and clean and sharpen tools

• Prolong the life of wooden garden furniture with a coat of teak oil or preservative, clean off any grime on synthetic furniture, and remove rust

from metal furniture

🍑 Prune newly planted apple and pear trees to encourage a well-branched, open shape, and carry out regular pruning of established trees

EARLY SPRING

The first faint flush of new growth in spring is a signal that the garden is finally stirring from its winter sleep. Time for the gardener to stir, too, and get down to some essential spring tasks. Feeding and mulching the garden take high priority, along with completing any outstanding plantings; neglected lawns too will benefit from a spring rejuvenation programme. Many shrubs should now be pruned, to keep them shapely and encourage better flowering, and a whole host of plants can be started from seed. There is plenty to do, but it is pleasant, quick and easy work on a fine spring day.

▲ *Planting perennials (here, hosta) is a key task for early spring.*

PLANTING HARDY PERENNIALS

 !!! 5 MINS PER PLANT

• **Perennials are invaluable for long-term flower and foliage interest**
• **They require a minimum of care once established**
• **Many will tolerate difficult conditions such as dry shade**

Hardy perennials are any non-woody plants that can be grown outdoors year round without any protection. They may be deciduous and die back in winter – delphiniums and hostas, for example – or evergreen, such as hellebores and many ferns. Perennials are the mainstay of any garden, providing many months of colour and interest in return for a minimum of care. A spring planting gives them a chance to get established before drier weather sets in, and it is also a useful time for planting slightly tender perennials, such as penstemon, giving the young plants time to toughen up before they face their first winter.

■ If spring planting is not possible, the other optimum time for planting is mid- to late autumn.

TIPS

❀ Try to avoid planting hardy perennials in the drier summer months. They will need constant time-consuming watering to see them through any long hot spells.

❀ Pot-grown, clump-forming perennials, such as hostas and grasses, can often be divided up before planting (*see p.109*), providing extra plants at no additional cost.

❀ For healthy, trouble-free plants, always follow the soil and aspect guidelines on the label.

1 Water the plant thoroughly, then make a hole twice the width of the root ball. If the soil is poor, dig in plenty of organic matter such as well-rotted manure before planting.

2 Remove the plant from the container (here, hosta) and gently tease out the outer roots and any that are growing in circles around the root ball, to encourage a wide-rooting habit.

3 Set the plant in so that the top of the compost is flush with the soil. Fill in with soil around the root ball, taking care not to create any air pockets, and firm down. Water well.

PLANTING WALL SHRUBS AND CLIMBERS

  ! ! ! 15–20 MINS PER PLANT

• **Planting against walls widens the range of shrubs you can grow, to include those that are slightly tender**

• **Spring planting gives them plenty of time to establish over summer**

Many of the most popular shrubs, including ceanothus, hebes and fremontodendrons, benefit from the extra protection of a wall, especially in colder climates. Adding organic matter when planting is essential, to improve water retention.

■ Wall plants that are totally hardy, such as climbing roses, can also be planted in mid- to late autumn.

TIPS

❀ It is vital to water plants thoroughly before planting. If the root ball is dry, they can take weeks longer to establish in the soil, regardless of how much water is provided after planting.

❀ The easiest of the wall shrubs are those that are free-standing and need no additional support, such as pyracantha, ceanothus and escallonia. Similarly, self-clinging climbers save the time and trouble of training them against trellis or wire. They include ivy (*Hedera*), climbing hydrangea (*Hydrangea anomala* subsp. *petiolaris*) and Virginia creepers (*Parthenocissus*).

❀ Clematis are exceptional in that they should always be planted 10cm (4in) deeper than they were in the pot (*see p.92*), so that they can regenerate from underground stems if clematis wilt strikes.

❀ Keep newly planted wall shrubs and climbers well watered through dry spells in their first spring and summer.

▶ *Ceanothus (here, 'Autumnal Blue') is one of the many shrubs that benefit from the protection of a wall.*

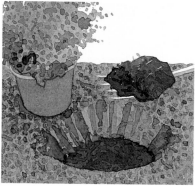

1 Dig a planting hole twice the width and depth of the container, siting it at least 40cm (16in) away from the base of the wall, to avoid the driest area. Mix the excavated soil with rich organic matter, such as well-rotted manure.

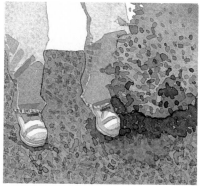

2 Soak the plant (here, rhododendron), remove from the container and tease out any congested roots. Line the hole with the soil mix and set the plant in so that it is just slightly below soil level. Fill in with the soil mix and firm down.

3 Scrape away a little of the soil around the plant to create a shallow depression. This will make watering much more efficient by channelling water directly to the roots. Saturate the plant and surrounding soil.

4 Spread a 5–8cm (2–3in) layer of mulch, such as bark chips or cocoa shell, over the surrounding soil. This will help the plant to establish much more quickly by conserving moisture and smothering weeds.

PLANTING ALPINES IN WALLS AND CREVICES

  5 MINS PER PLANT

• **Wall planting is a lovely way to display some of the easiest, most undemanding alpines**

Dry-stone walls and rock crevices provide ideal free-draining conditions for a wide range of alpine plants, including saxifrages and sedums, in all their wonderful diversity of leaf and flower, lewisias, rockery pinks (*Dianthus*) and many of the pretty alpine campanulas.

TIPS

✿ A paving weeder makes quick work of cleaning out crevices.

✿ To prevent plants from drying out, use a mist-spray to provide moisture, spraying daily in dry weather until they are growing strongly.

✿ Well-rooted plants can be difficult to insert into walls and crevices, and some damage is inevitable. Small plants from the garden centre, or rooted cuttings, will make the job much easier.

▲ *Sempervivums (here,* S. ciliosum *var.* borisii*) make ideal wall plants and will eventually spread into cushion-like clumps.*

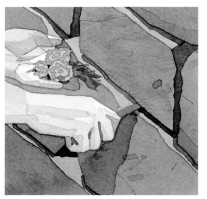

1 Water the plant (here, sempervivum), then gently remove most of the compost from the roots. Clean out the crevice to make a small planting hole.

2 Lay the plant on a narrow trowel or folded card and carefully feed the roots into the crevice until the plant is flush with the wall face.

3 Pack moist compost into the crevice until the plant is firmly anchored in position. Wedging in a few small stones will help to retain the compost.

TOP-DRESSING THE ROCK GARDEN

  5 MINS PER SQ M/YD

• **Replacing the top-dressing keeps alpine beds looking good, and promotes healthy plant growth**

Top-dressing, together with a gritty soil or compost, provides ideal growing conditions for alpines.

TIP

✿ Tucking top-dressing under plants keeps their 'collars' dry and free from rot, saving the time and expense of replacing failed plants.

1 Working carefully round the plants with a trowel, scrape away the old top-dressing, at the same time removing a thin layer of soil or compost.

2 Add fresh soil or compost, and top up with gravel or other top-dressing, tucking it under the base of cushion-forming plants (here, saxifrage).

SPRING FEEDING AND MULCHING

  !!! 1 HOUR PER 5 SQ M/YD ●

• **Feeding promotes strong-growing plants that are much more resistant to pest and disease attack**

• **Mulches, among their other virtues, are a quick and easy no-dig method of keeping the soil in excellent condition**

Feeding the garden in spring is a vital task and will ensure that plants grow strongly when the weather warms. If you let them go hungry, they will never reach their full potential and are much more susceptible to pests and diseases, which involve time and effort to eradicate. Mulching the garden is equally beneficial. Applied when the soil is moist, mulches lock in moisture, keep the soil cooler in summer, smother weeds, and make a good soil conditioner once they have broken down. Proprietary mulches include cocoa shell and various grades of bark, but you can also use any good organic matter such as spent mushroom compost.

TIPS

❀ Some gardeners like to dig the mulch into the top few centimetres of soil, but this is unnecessary – worms will come to the surface and drag it down for you.

❀ Well-rotted manure can be bought loose, but this involves a good deal of barrowing to and fro from the site where it is tipped. In smaller gardens, the rather more expensive bagged manures will save a good deal of time and effort.

❀ Mushroom compost makes an excellent mulch, but it contains lime and should therefore not be applied to lime-hating plants such as azaleas and rhododendrons.

▶ *All plants (here, euonymous) benefit from annual feeding and mulching.*

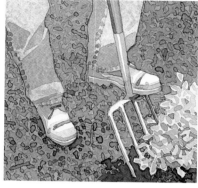

1 When the soil is moist, loosen the top few centimetres with a fork, taking care not to disturb shallow-rooted plants. This avoids the necessity of raking in fertilizers, and helps mulches to 'bind' more easily with the soil.

2 Apply a general fertilizer to all of the plants at the recommended rate, not to let it come into contact with the leaves or stems. Scattering the granules in a circle around the plant encourages spreading root growth.

3 To mulch the plants, tip the mulching material out of the barrow or bag and spread it around the plants with a rake or garden fork. To provide effective cover, the finished layer of mulch should be at least 8cm (3in) thick.

4 Spread the mulch to the full extent of the canopy of young trees and shrubs, making sure to leave a gap around the stem. If the mulch is in direct contact with the wood, the extra moisture can cause rotting.

PRUNING SHRUBS FOR SHAPE AND FLOWERS

  !!! 10–15 MINS PER SHRUB

• **Hard pruning keeps vigorous plants like buddleja and lavatera under control, ensuring a shapely plant and prolific flowering**
• **A lighter prune encourages the production of fresh flowering wood on shrubs like summer-flowering spiraeas and hypericum**

Shrubs that flower on this year's new stems benefit greatly from annual pruning. It encourages vigorous fresh growth, bearing more, and better, flowers. Lavatera and the vigorous forms of buddleja, such as *B. davidii*, very quickly develop into top-heavy, ungainly bushes, putting on several metres of growth each year. Hard pruning is essential to keep them looking good. Other shrubs that regularly produce new stems from the base benefit from being thinned out and trimmed back, to encourage a neat habit and plenty of flowers. They include caryopteris, hypericum and *Spiraea japonica*.

TIPS

✿ Prune as early in spring as possible to allow the maximum time for flowering stems to develop.

✿ Make a straight cut across the stem of shrubs such as buddleja, which bear buds in opposite pairs – both buds will then grow on. Make a slanting cut on shrubs which produce alternate buds, angling it down and away from the bud.

✿ Water well after pruning and feed and mulch if this was not done earlier (*see p.17*) to promote rapid and vigorous new growth.

✿ Use shears to cut back slim-stemmed plants such as hypericum.

▶ *Annual pruning is vital for the more vigorous buddlejas, such as B. 'Lochinch'.*

1 To keep buddleja (shown here) and lavatera in trim, first cut out any of the older branches that are causing congestion or are awkwardly placed. Cut them almost flush with the main stem, using loppers if they are very thick.

2 Using secateurs, cut back the remaining stems to within two or three buds of the previous season's growth. If new replacement stems are emerging from the base, cut them back by half to encourage a branching habit.

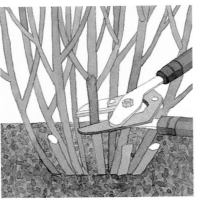

1 To shape up summer-flowering spiraeas and other similar shrubs, first cut out up to one-third of the main stems to the base. This will open up the framework of the plant, and will help encourage vigorous replacement growth.

2 Using secateurs, trim back all of the remaining main stems by approximately half, cutting just above an outward-facing leaf bud, then tidy them up by removing any damaged, twiggy or awkwardly placed growth.

PRUNING BUSH ROSES

  !!! 5–10 MINS PER PLANT ▶

• Rose pruning is a quick and easy job once the basic rules are mastered, promoting good health and maximum vigour
• It produces shapely plants with good leaf cover and optimum flowers from one of the most valued of all plants for summer colour and scent

Large-flowered (hybrid tea) and cluster-flowered (floribunda) roses flower on the current season's wood, and need fairly drastic pruning to give of their best. If left unpruned they develop into ungainly bushes with fewer, and smaller, flowers.

■ Shrub roses, flowering on the older wood, are much less time-consuming. After flowering, cut back woodier stems by a quarter, trim off any untidy or damaged growth, and take out one or two of the older main stems every few years to encourage new growth.

TIPS

❀ Spring rose pruning should be undertaken when the plants are still dormant, or when buds are just breaking. If pruning while dormant, the potential buds are identifiable as a slight horizontal 'scar' on the stem. Never prune in frosty conditions.

❀ For quick and easy pruning of patio and miniature roses, shear them over to around 15cm (6in) of the ground. It may seem brutal, but the shorn stems are soon hidden by the new growth.

❀ Ground-cover roses, with their naturally neat habit, need pruning only to curtail their spread.

▶ *Fragrant 'Just Joey' is one of the loveliest of the large-flowered roses.*

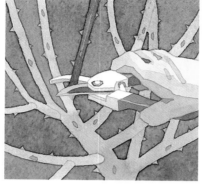

1 Using secateurs, cut out dead or damaged wood, and any that shows signs of disease. Stems sometimes start to die back from the tip, turning a blackish brown. Cut them back 5cm (2in) or so into the living wood.

2 Remove any spindly or twiggy growth, cutting it right back to the main stem. If left unpruned, it will congest the plant, impede good air circulation, and divert energy from plumper, more productive shoots.

3 Open out the centre of the bush by removing any congested or crossing growth. Aim for an open goblet shape, so that air and sunshine reach all parts of the plant, promoting good health and optimum flowering.

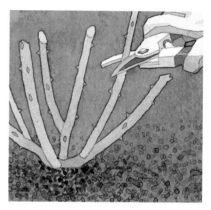

4 Reduce the remaining stems to around 25cm (10in) from ground level. To achieve the ideal goblet shape, always cut above an outward-facing bud, slanting the cut away from it. Feed and mulch (*see p.17*) after pruning.

PRUNING SHRUBS FOR STEM AND LEAF COLOUR

  !! | 5–10 MINS PER SHRUB | ▶

- **A quick, annual pruning will guarantee the freshest, brightest stem and leaf colour**
- **It is an easy way to keep vigorous trees, such as eucalyptus, in check so that they can be grown in even the smallest garden**

Some shrubs and trees respond well to very severe pruning, producing new growth that is much more colourful than that of unpruned specimens. The dogwoods (*Cornus*), grown for their coloured bark, very soon lose their brightness and lustre if they are left unpruned, as do the ornamental white-stemmed brambles like *Rubus cockburnianus*. Cutting back *Eucalyptus gunnii* promotes the growth of the much-prized, silvery juvenile foliage, while the attractive gold-leaved forms of elder (*Sambucus*) and catalpa produce larger, more brightly coloured leaves if they are cut back hard.

 TIPS

❀ Some dogwoods are valued for their variegated leaves together with the coloured stems. Cut out only one-third of the stems of these varieties, to ensure a good leaf cover in summer.

❀ Always feed and mulch well after pruning (*see p.17*).

▶ *The cherry-red stems of* Cornus alba *'Westonbirt' gleam in the winter sun.*

Hard prune dogwoods by cutting stems back to within approximately 10cm (4in) of the base, to ensure brightly coloured new growth through summer and to provide interest in winter.

Using loppers, cut eucalyptus back to within 5–8cm (2–3in) of the main stem to stimulate the production of the more attractive juvenile foliage, which is highly prized for flower arrangements.

RENOVATING A HONEYSUCKLE

  !! | 30 MINS PER PLANT | ◑

- **A simple operation that quickly rejuvenates tired, overgrown plants**

Honeysuckles (*Lonicera*) are invaluable climbers, but can become unsightly, with a tangled mass of unproductive old stems.

 TIP

❀ Check the eventual height when choosing a honeysuckle. Those that grow to only 4–5m (12–15ft) will be much easier to keep under control. *Lonicera* x *tellmanniana* (a coppery orange) and *L.* x *brownii* 'Dropmore Scarlet' (in red) are two of the neatest.

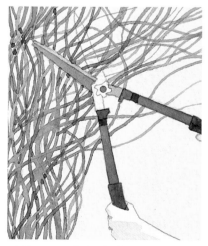

1 Cut away all the 'bird's nest' tangle of growth, taking it right back to the main stems. Speed up the job by using shears rather than secateurs on the twiggier outer growth.

2 Cut the main stems back to within 30–60cm (1–2ft) of the ground, using loppers. Feed, water and mulch around the base (*see p.17*). New shoots soon appear and can be trained in.

SOWING BORDER ANNUALS

  10 MINS PER SQ M/YD

• **Annuals are an easy, colourful way to fill spare ground in summer, especially in a bed newly planted with young shrubs and perennials**
• **This sowing method makes quick work of weeding since weeds are easy to identify and control**

Hardy and half-hardy annuals are lovely gap-fillers, and this method of sowing really maximizes their potential. By sowing in straight lines, seedling plants are instantly recognizable, and seedling weeds can be hoed or pulled out as soon as they emerge. In addition, the interlocking sowing areas create a series of flowing drifts for a natural, unified effect. Hardy varieties can be sown now, and half-hardy annuals within the next few weeks as advised on the seed packet. The young plants will look rather regimented at first, but soon they will knit together to form a solid mass of leaf and flower.

TIPS

❀ To ensure a harmonious, well-balanced planting, make a rough sowing plan before marking out the seed bed, noting plant heights and flower colour.

❀ The old 'cottage garden' annuals are some of the easiest to grow from seed. They include candytuft (*Iberis*), clarkia, pot marigold (*Calendula*), cornflower (*Centaurea cyanus*) and love-in-a-mist (*Nigella*).

❀ Border annuals do not need any regular feeding, but if the soil is very impoverished, rake in a balanced fertilizer at 70g per sq m (2oz per sq yd) before sowing.

▶ *Pretty love-in-a-mist* (Nigella) *is one of the easiest of 'cottage garden' annuals.*

1 To make the seed bed, fork the soil well, breaking up any lumps or clods, then rake to create a fine, crumbly surface. Using silver sand or pale grit, mark out a series of interlocking sowing areas for individual varieties.

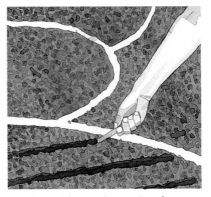

2 Use a stick to make a series of small seed drills within the marked area, spacing them according to the recommended sowing distance on the packet, so that plants grow together well without being overcrowded.

3 Sow the seed when the soil is moist, spacing it as evenly as possible (fine seed can be mixed with sand to help with distribution). Cover the seed with soil, tamp it down, using the back of a rake, and label clearly.

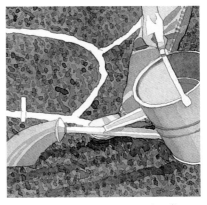

4 Water well, using a can with a fine rose, and keep watered through any dry spells. When the seedlings emerge, thin them to the distance recommended on the seed packet, and remove any weed seedlings between drills.

PROPAGATING SHRUBS BY LAYERING

   10–15 MINS PER SHRUB

• **Layering is a good way to increase stock of the more expensive shrubs such as rhododendrons, azaleas and magnolias**

• **Unlike other propagation methods, once the initial layering operation is complete, very little aftercare is needed**

The process of layering mimics the natural habit of many shrubs – rooting from a stem where it touches the ground. A wide range of evergreen and deciduous shrubs can be propagated by layering, including most of the rhododendron family, lilac (*Syringa*), skimmia, viburnums and magnolias. It is a method that is always worth trying with any shrub, since it requires a minimal outlay of time and money. Layered stems normally root within a year, and can be transplanted the following spring or autumn.

■ Layering can also be undertaken in mid- to late autumn.

TIPS

❀ Keep the ground around the layer well watered in dry weather. Leave layered stems for at least a year.

❀ Before transplanting, gently fork around the layer to check that a good root system has developed.

❀ An even quicker method of layering, though not so foolproof, is simply to place a brick over the stem where it brushes the ground.

❀ Many climbers, including honeysuckle (*Lonicera*) and wisteria, can also be propagated by layering. It is a particularly useful way to propagate clematis, which can be difficult to grow from cuttings.

▶ *Rhododendrons (here, 'Seta') can be costly, but are easy to propagate by layering.*

1 Select a whippy stem close to the base of the shrub (here, rhododendron). Trim off the leaves along the stem, about 30cm (1ft) behind the growing tip. Bend the stem to the ground to mark the position where it will be buried.

2 Dig a small trench to a spade's width and half a spade's depth. If the soil is poor, mix plenty of organic matter with the excavated soil to help retain moisture, and create optimum rooting conditions for the layered portion.

3 Using a sharp knife, cut a 2–5cm (1–2in) 'tongue' of bark along the underside of the stem at the point where it touches the ground, cutting no more than half way into the stem. This slight wound helps stimulate rooting.

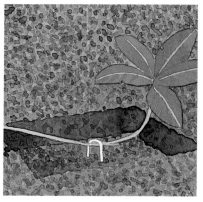

4 Peg the stem down so that the wounded section is in contact with the soil. Fill in, firm down well and water thoroughly. When the layer has rooted and is growing strongly, sever from the parent and transplant.

TAKING BASAL STEM CUTTINGS

  ! 15 MINS PER POT

• **A quick and easy way to propagate hardy chrysanthemums, delphiniums, lupins and dahlias, taking advantage of the vigour of the young spring shoots**
• **Rooted cuttings will be ready to plant out by late spring or early summer, and will often flower in the same year**

Basal stem cuttings root remarkably quickly (usually within a month), because the first rush of spring growth has great vigour, and the resulting young plants will often flower in their first year. It is an exceptionally quick and easy way to increase stocks of popular plants such as border chrysanthemums, delphiniums, lupins, dahlias and bergamot (*Monarda*).

New cuttings should be potted up as quickly as possible. If you are taking several at a time, it is best to seal them in a polythene bag straight away, to prevent them from wilting. If they do wilt, place them in water until they have revived.

When the rooted cuttings have been potted up individually, place them in a warm, light position indoors away from direct sun to grow on. Although you should keep the cuttings well watered, be sure they are not over-moist.

In mid- to late spring, start to acclimatize the cuttings by placing them outside on warmer days, bringing them in at night. As the weather warms, gradually increase the time they spend outdoors, leaving them out on frost-free nights. Plant the cuttings out when all danger of frost has passed, and keep them well watered until they are growing strongly.

TIPS

✿ Be sparing when dipping cuttings into hormone rooting powder; too much can be harmful.

✿ For ultra-quick rooting of basal stem cuttings, use a heated propagator, removing the lid when they are growing strongly.

✿ Keep the compost evenly moist but not saturated; moisture build-up can cause rot. If condensation forms, wipe the propagator lid, or remove the polythene bag for a few hours to allow it to disperse.

▲ *Border chrysanthemums will offer a welcome splash of colour in autumn.*

1 Wait until the plant (here, border chrysanthemum) has produced shoots approximately 5cm (2in) long. Select a healthy, sturdy shoot and cut it off as close to the base as possible, where the stem is just beginning to become woody.

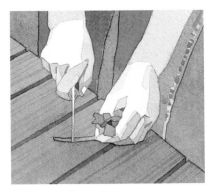

2 Prepare the cuttings as soon as possible after taking them. Using a sharp knife, trim off the lower leaves and make a straight cut across the base of the stem, so that approximately 1cm (½in) of the woodier material is retained.

3 Dip the ends of the stems in hormone rooting powder and, using a dibber, insert the cuttings around the edge of a pot of cuttings compost. Space the cuttings so that the leaves of adjacent plants are not touching.

4 Water moderately and place the pot in a clear polythene bag secured with an elastic band. Set it in a warm, light position indoors, away from direct sun. When the cuttings have rooted, pot them on individually.

GROWING ON OVERWINTERED TENDER PERENNIALS

  | 5–10 MINS PER PLANT ▶

• **Overwintered tender perennials will be well into their flowering stride by the time they are planted out in early summer**

• **These fairly mature plants save time and money by reducing the number of bedding plants needed to fill summer pots and baskets**

Many tender perennials can be overwintered indoors (*see p.86*), to provide relatively large plants for instant colour and impact in bedding schemes, pots and borders from early summer. Most keep on growing slowly through winter, although marguerites (*Argyranthemum*) and fuchsias go dormant, putting out new growth in spring. All can be grown on in the same way as geraniums (*Pelargonium*). Use a good multi-purpose compost when potting up, and feed plants weekly from mid-spring, using a fertilizer suitable for flowering bedding plants.

TIPS

❀ To spur plants into action before repotting, gradually increase watering. Water them when the the compost has started to dry out, but always dispose of any water that has drained through into the plant saucer after half an hour or so.

❀ Woody perennials, such as marguerites and fuchsias, can be pruned back hard to 5cm (2in), to create densely bushy plants.

❀ Save time on hanging basket and window box plants by potting them up direct – just bring the container indoors, put in the plants, fill in with other summer bedding, and grow on in warm, light conditions.

▶ *Free-flowering and vigorous, geraniums (Pelargonium) are ideal bedding plants.*

1 Repot the overwintered plant (here, geranium) into a slightly larger pot, easing in fresh compost and firming down. If using a terracotta pot, line the base with crocks to ensure good drainage. Water well.

2 Using secateurs, cut the older, woodier stems right back to encourage vigorous new stems from the base. These will create a balanced plant that is well furnished with leaves and flowers from top to bottom.

3 Cut back the remaining younger stems by half, making the cut above an outward-facing leaf joint, so that the resulting new growth forms a globe shape, leaving the centre of the plant open and uncongested.

4 Set the plant in a warm, bright position indoors, keeping it evenly moist but not wet. As it grows, pinch out the stem tips to encourage a densely bushy habit. Plant out when all danger of frost has passed.

PATIO SPRING CLEAN

 !!! | 1 HOUR PER 10 SQ M/YD | ●

• **A quick clean-up improves the look of any paved area, providing a smart backdrop for planted pots and garden furniture**
• **It keeps maintenance to a minimum for the rest of the year**

It is surprising how dirt, algae and weeds can build up on the patio, often without the gardener taking notice of the gradual deterioration. A spring clean-up makes a cheering difference, especially on light-coloured paving, which will be returned to sparkling form. It is especially important to remove the algal film that builds up in shady areas, because it becomes very slippery when wet and quite a hazard, particularly if the paving borders a pond. Removing weeds keeps the whole area neat, and brings patterned paving back into focus. Weeding early, before plants have set seed, significantly reduces the need to weed later in the year.

TIPS

❀ For quick weeding, wait until the ground is moist and weeds release their grip quite easily. Weeds are always more difficult to remove in dry conditions.

❀ The easiest way to prevent weeds in paving cracks is to brush in a dry cement mix. It is available from hardware and DIY stores, and once watered it sets to form an impenetrable barrier.

❀ Before using a jet sprayer, remove any pots from the patio to protect them from dirty spray splashes. To protect yourself, wear goggles, gumboots and old clothes.

▶ *Clean, weed-free paving is the perfect setting for planted pots.*

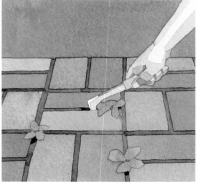

A sharp knife can be used to prise weeds out of paving cracks, but a special paving weeder, which hooks under the roots, is the ideal way to get rid of shallow-rooted weeds such as grass and daisies.

To clean off dirt and algae, scrub the paving with a stiff garden broom and soapy water, and rinse thoroughly. If a proprietary patio cleaner is preferred, make sure that it does not leach into any nearby borders or ponds.

For deeper-rooted weeds, such as dandelions, and in areas where there are no cultivated plants in the surrounding paving, spray with a weedkiller containing glyphosate, which is completely harmless once dry.

To save time on larger areas of paving, use a high-pressure jet spray, which will blast off the dirt at a remarkable rate. These machines can be expensive, but are readily available from hire shops.

SOWING SEED INDOORS

  5 MINS PER POT

• Sowing seed indoors is an easy way to raise a whole range of plants that need a little extra warmth for germination
• It cuts costs dramatically – a single packet of seed can contain tens, and sometimes hundreds, of potential plants
• After the initial outlay on equipment, the only ongoing expenses are seed and compost

Growing plants from seed can be very satisfying and it certainly keeps down the costs, especially if you are a keen vegetable gardener, or like to indulge in a good display of bedding plants each year. Hardy plants can be sown *in situ* outdoors (*see pp.21 and 29*), but sowing in heat gives you access to all those plants that need extra warmth for germination: many perennial border plants, tender varieties of bedding plants and tender herbs and vegetables.

Bedding plants are one of the most popular subjects for indoor sowings, since the vast majority are dependent on heat for germination. Some are easier to raise from seed than others, however. Busier gardeners might like to concentrate on the following extra-easy varieties that do not need careful temperature control to guarantee good germination: bidens, brachyscome, dahlias, diascias, felicia, gazania, marigolds (*Calendula* and *Tagetes*), nasturtium (*Tropaeolum*), nemesia, nolana, osteospermum, portulaca, and tobacco plants (*Nicotiana*).

Using a heated propagator is certainly the easiest way to stimulate

▶ *Seed of compact, free-flowering semperflorens begonias is widely available.*

1 Fill a pot or seed tray with seed and cutting compost, level it off and firm down to within 1cm (½in) of the rim. If using a terracotta pot, first line the base with crocks or gravel to prevent the drainage hole from becoming blocked.

2 Sow the seed as evenly as possible, lightly shaking it from the packet. If the seed is very fine and dust-like, add silver sand to the packet, shake to mix, then spread the mix to give a more even distribution.

3 Cover the seed with vermiculite or compost to the depth advised on the seed packet. The use of vermiculite, a lightweight material that retains warmth and moisture, appears to benefit germination rates.

4 Label and water so that the compost is evenly moist but not saturated. Use a can fitted with a fine rose for gentle watering – a jet of water will disturb the compost and the carefully distributed seed.

germination, but you can also just wrap the pot or tray in a polythene bag after sowing, and place it in the airing cupboard, or on top of the central heating boiler. As soon as the seedlings emerge, remove the polythene and place the pot or tray on a warm, well-lit windowsill out of direct sun. If it is on a windowsill, you will find that the seedlings tend to bend towards the light, so turn the pot or tray every so often so that they do not develop a permanent lean.

It is best to water all but the largest, most vigorous seedlings from below, because even when using a watering can fitted with a fine rose, tender seedlings can be knocked over by the sheer force of the water. Stand the pot or tray in a shallow bowl of water, and allow it to soak until the surface of the compost is moist, then leave it to drain for several minutes. If your tap water is very cold, you should wait until it has reached room temperature before beginning to water the seedlings.

Transferring seedlings to modules to grow on until planting-out time cuts down the work involved in growing smaller bedding plants, since the alternative method would be to transfer them first to a seed tray to grow on for a while, and then to individual pots.

In mid-spring, start to acclimatize the young plants to garden temperatures. Place them in a sheltered spot on warm sunny days, gradually increasing the time that they spend outdoors until they can eventually be left out overnight – unless frost is forecast. Plant the seedlings out in the open garden, or in containers, after the danger of frost has passed.

5 Place the pots in a heated propagator and set in a well-lit position away from direct sun. If moisture builds up inside the lid, open the ventilators to disperse it; seedlings are susceptible to rot in damp conditions.

6 Water if the compost starts to dry out, and when seedlings emerge, gradually open the vents to acclimatize them to drier air, then finally remove the lid. Grow on until a second set of leaves has developed.

7 To transplant the seedlings, use a dibber to ease the roots out of the compost. Hold the seedlings by a seed leaf (the first, more sturdy set of leaves) – never handle them by the stems, which are brittle and break very easily.

8 Transfer each seedling to a separate module of a plant pack, using the dibber to make a hole in the compost. Ease the roots in, firm down and water well. Place in a warm, light position to grow on, and keep evenly moist.

TIPS

❀ Some seed should not be covered after sowing, so always check the packet instructions. To prevent this seed from being washed into the compost, always water from below.

❀ Larger seeds, such as beans or melons, can be sown two to a 9cm (3½in) pot. When the seedlings emerge, gently ease out the weaker of the two, leaving the stronger plant to grow on.

❀ If seedlings are kept in over-moist conditions, they can suffer from 'damping off' – a sudden collapse caused by a fungus at the root. Remove any affected seedlings together with the compost around their roots, and grow on the remaining seedlings in drier, airier conditions.

❀ When transplanting seedlings to plant packs, choose a module size that corresponds to the plant variety. Dainty lobelia, for example, needs only small modules, while vigorous, tobacco plants (*Nicotiana*) require considerably more space, for their spreading foliage.

LAWN RENOVATION

  !! 1 HOUR PER 10 SQ M/YD ●

• Spring renovation creates a vigorous, healthy lawn that is better able to withstand the wear and tear of summer
• Aeration relieves compaction and waterlogging
• Raking, or scarifying, removes unsightly moss and eliminates the smothering surface thatch of dried grass

When the lawn starts to look tired and sparse, and the grass is struggling to grow despite regular feeding, a renovation programme can bring it back to life remarkably quickly. The aim of the renovation is to remove any moss or old dead grass, and to open up the soil and relieve compaction, so that the grass is better able to take up moisture and nutrients. It is hard work, but worth it when you see it greening up and thickening out within weeks.

■ Lawn renovation can also be undertaken in mid-autumn.

TIPS

❀ Kill off any moss a week or so before scarifying, to prevent it from spreading to other areas.

❀ For ultra-quick work on larger lawns, it is possible to hire an electric scarifier or aerator.

❀ If the season has been unexpectedly warm and the grass is more than 8cm (3in) high, mow it lightly (*see p.35*) before aerating and top-dressing.

❀ Save time and effort on aeration by waiting until the soil is moist. Heavy or compacted soils are very difficult to penetrate when dry.

▶ *Spring renovation encourages lush, vigorous lawn growth.*

1 Use a spring-tined rake to remove any moss and thatch (the layer of dead grass clippings that can build up on the surface of the soil), raking vigorously across the grass. Both moss and thatch deprive the grass of air and moisture.

2 Use a hollow-tined aerator to open up the soil, plunging it in at 10cm (4in) intervals to lift out narrow plugs of soil. This helps to relieve compaction, which can weaken grass growth, and allows water to penetrate more easily.

3 To improve the condition of the soil, use a besom or broom to brush a top-dressing – either a proprietary brand or good organic matter – into the holes made by the aerator. On heavier soils, add sand or fine grit to aid drainage.

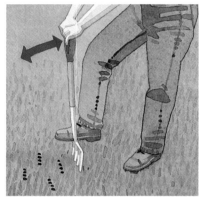

❀ On smaller lawns, a garden fork will do the job of aeration just as well as a hollow-tiner. Drive it in to approximately half the length of the prongs, every 10cm (4in). Gently rock it back and forth to enlarge the holes.

SOWING VEGETABLES IN ROWS

 ! 10 MINS PER 2M (6FT) ROW

• **Ultra-fresh vegetables are packed with goodness and flavour**
• **Direct sowing is the ideal way to grow root crops, such as carrots, which resent disturbance**
• **The space between rows can be used for quick-maturing 'catch crops', such as spring onions**

Sowing vegetables is simple, undemanding work, and the resulting crops, with minimal time between harvest and the plate, have premium flavour. They can be sown in a seed bed from which the young plants will be transplanted, or directly into the rows where they are to grow. The direct sowing method cuts out the time involved in transplanting, and is particularly useful for root crops such as beetroot, carrots and parsnip which do not transplant well. For a succession of crops, rather than a glut, sow individual crops at fortnightly intervals.

TIPS

❀ Grow vegetables in a sunny spot – very few are tolerant of shade.

❀ Always check the seed packet for the recommended sowing time. Delay sowing if the weather is unseasonably cold or if the ground is waterlogged.

❀ Protect seedlings and young plants from slugs and snails (*see p.125*), which can do considerable damage.

❀ Make use of the space between rows of slow-growing vegetables, such as parsnips, by 'catch-cropping' – sowing fast-maturing crops such as lettuces, radishes and spring onions, which can be harvested within weeks.

▶ *A well-tended plot can produce bumper crops of delicious vegetables.*

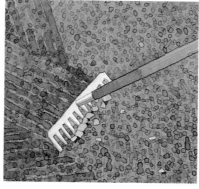

1 On level, well-prepared ground (*see p.107*), rake the surface of the soil to a fine, crumbly texture, removing any large stones; smaller stones are beneficial, helping to retain a little extra moisture, and providing slightly cooler conditions.

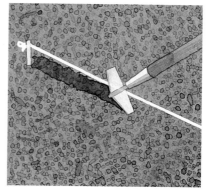

2 Carefully mark out the rows at the recommended spacing distance, using pegs or canes and tightly stretched line. With the corner of a hoe, make a neat, V-shaped seed drill to the required depth, using the line as a guide.

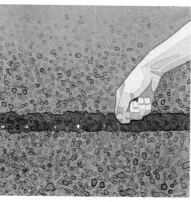

3 Water the drill if the soil is dry, then sow the seed as evenly as possible – finer seed can be mixed with horticultural sand to help give a more even distribution. Firm the soil over the drill, label it clearly and water thoroughly.

4 When the seedlings emerge, carefully thin them to the recommended spacing, taking care not to disturb other seedlings in the row. Keep seedlings well watered in dry weather, and hoe or pull any weed seedlings.

MID-SPRING

Mid-spring can be blowy, blustery and often wet, but it always has its fair share of fine sunny days which make gardening a real pleasure, so take full advantage of them. As the weather warms, hedges will probably need a trim and the lawn its first cut. New lawns can be created, after some careful ground preparation, and there is plenty to get on with in the vegetable garden, from planting potatoes to sowing carrots and lettuces for delicious late spring and summer crops. There may be a great deal to do at this time of the year – but there is also a lot to look forward to.

▲ *Stake peonies from an early stage to display the luscious flowers to best advantage.*

STAKING HERBACEOUS PERENNIALS

  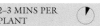 | 2–3 MINS PER PLANT |

• **Staking with canes keeps tall flower stems sturdily upright**
• **A ring stake is the ideal way to display heavy-headed flowers**
• **Link stakes can protect lawn edges from being shaded out by floppy plants**

Many herbaceous perennials need staking – to keep tall flower stems on the straight and narrow; to tidy up plants with a floppy habit and stop them from encroaching on their neighbours or onto the lawn; and to support heavy-headed flowers, such as peonies and oriental poppies (*Papaver orientale*), which would otherwise bend earthward and lose their impact. The important thing to remember is that any staking should be discreet, so that the stakes do not intrude into the overall garden picture. They will be obvious in the early stages, but by summer they should have disappeared under a sea of foliage and flowers. Extra work, maybe – but well worth the effort for maximum enjoyment of some of the most valuable and desirable of summer flowers.

TIPS

❀ When staking a single-stemmed plant, use a cane that matches the eventual height of the plant: the cane must be tall enough to fully support the plant, but should not protrude.

❀ Woody pruned stems can be used to support bushy plants, pushed in among the young foliage. A circle of canes, linked together at the top with twine, makes an effective substitute for metal link stakes.

❀ Erecting a windbreak in exposed gardens can greatly reduce the need for staking plants.

Stake single-stemmed plants, such as delphiniums, using a stout cane. Tie in the flower stems at 30cm (1ft) intervals to prevent them from kinking or breaking in an exposed, windy situation.

Use ring stakes to support heavy-headed flowers such as peonies and oriental poppies. Raise the stake as the plant grows, and train the foliage and flower stems through the mesh.

Link stakes will constrain tall, clump-forming plants such as phlox. They will also prevent plants from flopping over onto the lawn. They may be linked in a circle or in a line.

BULB CARE AFTER FLOWERING

   5–10 MINS PER CLUMP

• Annual aftercare is quick and easy, promoting healthy, free-flowering bulbs that will form ever-increasing clumps and provide excellent spring displays, year after year

• It helps avoid the necessity of replanting areas where bulbs have failed through neglect

Bulbs bloom so well in their first few years that it is easy to assume that they need no care at all; however, a little annual aftercare is vital for successful displays year after year, and takes very little time. Removing spent blooms is essential, both to keep plants looking neat and to prevent them from setting seed, which drains vigour from the bulb. Letting the leaves die down naturally, and feeding after flowering, will also help to channel the maximum amount of energy back to the bulb, which is already beginning to form next year's flowers.

TIPS

❀ Bulbs in heavily planted borders need annual feeding after flowering, using a high-potash formulation, but bulbs in grass should be fed only if flowering starts to diminish. This stimulates flower production without benefiting the grass, which prefers a nitrogen-rich diet.

❀ Planting bulbs under deciduous shrubs or trees is the ideal solution to untidy foliage – the bulbs will flower while the shrub or tree is bare, and the developing foliage will help to hide the bulb's unsightly dying leaves.

❀ When growing bulbs in grass, use early varieties that will not delay the normal date for the first mowing.

▶ *Bulbs will increase in beauty year after year with just a little annual care.*

1 Remove flowers (here, daffodil) as they begin to fade, to prevent them from setting seed and draining energy from the bulb. Ideally, nip them off just below the seed pod, although whole stems can be removed if they look untidy.

2 Feed after flowering, using a balanced fertilizer to help plump up the bulb for maximum flower production next year. Quick-acting liquid feed, watered in around the plant or sprayed onto the foliage, is ideal.

3 Daffodil leaves, in particular, can look very untidy after flowering, but they should never be cut prematurely, or tied into knots. While the leaves are photosynthesizing, they are directing energy to the bulb.

4 When leaves have finally become floppy and yellowed (usually after six weeks or so), and are of no further use to the bulb, they can be cut back with shears. Do not pull the leaves off, as this can damage the bulb.

HEDGE TRIMMING

  !!! 10–20 MINS PER 6M (20FT) RUN

- **Regular trimming encourages a dense, even cover**
- **It creates a crisp outline that contrasts well with less formal garden plants**
- **This is satisfying work, because results are immediately visible**

A well-trimmed hedge is an asset in any garden – whether as a screen for privacy, or to divide the garden into 'compartments', it makes the perfect green backdrop for more colourful plants and flowers. Hedges are more time-consuming than fences, but will last indefinitely. To keep them in good shape, fully furnished with leaves from top to bottom, always cut them so that the base is wider than the top. This prevents the lower branches from being shaded out and dying back, deflects wind, and minimizes the impact of a heavy snowfall, which could break the branches of a broad-topped hedge.

TIPS

❀ Wear goggles when using hedge trimmers to protect your eyes from flying debris.

❀ Ear defenders block out the noise of a hedge trimmer, but others will still hear it, so trim at sociable times.

▶ *Regular trimming creates a neat, tight hedge such as this tapestry of beech.*

 When using shears, hold them parallel to the line of the hedge for an even finish, trimming it to a gently tapering shape. Lay a polythene sheet so that clippings can be gathered up easily.

If there are several hedges to be trimmed, powered hedge trimmers will save time and effort. To prevent accidents, always fit a power-breaking residual current device to the mains plug.

HEDGE RENOVATION

  !!! 1 HOUR PER 6M (20FT) RUN ●

- **Transforms overgrown hedges**

Most hedging plants respond well to renovation, although yew is the only conifer that can be cut hard back.
- Renovate deciduous hedges in late winter.

TIPS

❀ Loppers or a sharp saw will make short work of cutting back larger side branches.

❀ Feed, water and mulch thoroughly after cutting back to encourage vigorous new growth.

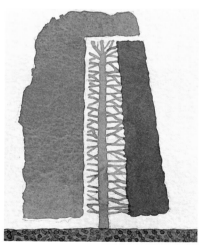

1 Trim the top of the hedge (here, yew) to 30cm (1ft) lower than the desired height, then cut back hard on one side only. Cut the other side to tidy it, leaving a good foliage cover.

2 When the cut side of the hedge has regenerated, and growth is dense and vigorous (usually after one or two years), it is safe to complete the renovation process by cutting back the other side.

PRUNING EVERGREEN SHRUBS AND CONIFERS

  !! 5–20 MINS PER PLANT

- Judicious pruning keeps plants shapely and promotes vigour by removing unproductive shoots
- Regular trimming keeps specimen plants looking neat and striking for year-round interest
- A quick annual shearing extends the life of lavenders and heathers, preventing them from becoming woody and leggy

Evergreens are invaluable garden plants, providing year-round structure and colour and requiring little maintenance. Most need pruning only if they have become unshapely, or have outgrown their allotted space. Mound-forming evergreens, such as lavenders and heathers, need just a quick annual trim. Conifers need no pruning at all, but can be lightly trimmed to create a neat finish.

■ Evergreens can be pruned up to midsummer, if necessary, but never in autumn or winter.

TIPS

❀ If an evergreen shrub has outgrown its allotted space, many will respond well to severe pruning. These include fatsia, euonymus, choisya, holly (*Ilex*) and the tiny-leaved shrubby honeysuckle, *Lonicera nitida*.

❀ Always feed, water and mulch after any drastic pruning (*see p.17*). This encourages vigorous new growth, which will ripen over summer and be much less susceptible to autumn and winter frosts.

❀ Suitable shrubs for clipping and training as specimens include holly, *Euonymus fortunei* hybrids, *Lonicera nitida*, box (*Buxus*), laurel (*Aucuba*), elaeagnus and bay (*Laurus*).

▶ *Like most evergreen shrubs, camellias require a minimum of pruning.*

Prune evergreen shrubs to remove dead or diseased growth, and any unproductive stems that are crowding the centre of the bush. Trim back any over-long or awkwardly placed stems that are spoiling the overall balance of the plant.

Many evergreen shrubs, such as holly and euonymus, make good formal specimens. Clip them over with shears every so often in midsummer to the required shape. A simple column, spire or dome is easy to maintain.

Trim back lavenders and heathers to remove the old flowers and create a neatly domed shape. Use light, single-handed shears for speed and ease. If plants are very straggly, trim them back by approximately one-third.

To tidy up conifers, clip them over lightly with shears when necessary. Never cut back into the stems to leave a leafless stump – conifers, with the exception of yew (*Taxus*), will not regenerate from bare wood.

CARE OF CONTAINER SHRUBS AND TREES

 !!! | 15–30 MINS PER POT | ◑

- **Container shrubs and trees enliven patios and paved areas and can provide a strong focal point**
- **Minimal maintenance is needed to keep plants in tip-top condition**

Container shrubs and trees are the backbone of any patio or paved area, giving it a fully furnished, established feel. All but the very largest trees and shrubs can be grown in containers, because the limited root run will restrict their size. Evergreens are particularly valuable, providing year-round interest, and there are plants to suit every situation – a tight conifer spire, for example, in a formal setting, or the huge, jungle-like leaves of *Fatsia japonica* for a tropical effect. Keeping these rewarding plants in good condition takes very little time, but is essential for their well-being.

■ Give plants a boost by feeding again in midsummer.

TIPS

❀ When repotting, use a pot only a little larger than the original.

❀ If acid-loving plants, such as rhododendrons or camellias, are looking jaded, use a fertilizer specially formulated for ericaceous plants.

❀ Never plant trees or shrubs in the Ali-Baba type of pot. When they need repotting it is virtually impossible to manoeuvre the root ball through the narrow neck.

Give container-grown shrubs and trees an instant boost as they come into growth in spring, by watering in a balanced, quick-release liquid fertilizer at the recommended rate.

1 Mature plants, which have reached their final pot size, benefit from an annual top-dressing. Carefully scrape away the top few centimetres of compost, taking care not to damage the roots.

2 Top up to the original level with loam-based compost or, for lime-haters such as azaleas, an ericaceous mix. Firm it down and water well. A mulch of gravel or bark chips will help retain moisture.

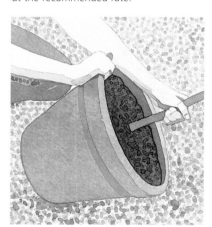

1 Younger plants will need to be potted on every 2–3 years. Water well an hour or so before repotting, to make the root ball easier to remove. Lay the pot on its side and carefully ease the plant out – a moist root ball is easier to remove.

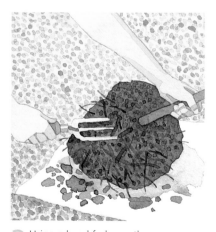

2 Using a hand fork, gently scrape away as much old compost as possible from around the roots, then carefully tease out any congested roots and those that are growing in circles around the root ball, taking care not to damage them.

3 Using a pot only one or two sizes larger than the original, place crocks in the base of the new pot, then add a layer of compost and position the plant centrally, spreading out the roots. Fill in with fresh compost and firm it down.

LAWNS – THE FIRST CUT

  20–30 MINS PER 100 SQ M/YD

• **Regular mowing creates a dense, even sward that smothers weeds and moss**

• **It discourages the growth of coarse grasses, allowing the finer grasses to flourish**

• **A neatly mown lawn keeps the whole garden looking good**

The lawn is an extremely important garden feature. It is a practical space, but also a quiet green oasis that highlights the colour, form and texture of surrounding plantings. An unkempt lawn can give the whole garden a dismal air, but a transformation takes place once it is neatly mown and edged, bringing everything into clearer, sharper focus. Regular mowing also encourages the grass to thicken up, smothering troublesome weeds and reducing the risk of disease. The height of cut depends on the type of grass – from 5cm (2in) for coarse grass, to 5mm (¼in) for the finest lawns.

TIPS

❀ Worm casts may be a nuisance, but worms are invaluable, aerating the soil to create better drainage and good growing conditions.

❀ Save time by choosing the right mower. A hover mower, for instance, copes well on an uneven surface, while the greater cutting width of large powered mowers makes quick work of more extensive lawns.

❀ If edging the lawn is taking up a good deal of time, it might be worth considering installing a 'mowing strip' – an edging of brick or paving set flush with the grass. The mower can simply be run onto the paved strip to remove edge grass.

▶ *A regularly mown lawn provides the perfect setting for colourful beds and borders.*

1 If there are worm casts on the lawn, scatter them with a besom. If they are damp, lift them carefully with a trowel to avoid leaving muddy smears when mowing. Never kill worms – they are invaluable for aerating the soil.

2 For the first few cuts, set the blades higher than normal and collect the grass clippings by fitting a grass box or by raking them up. Alternatively, use a mulching mower (*see p.71*), which will shred them extra-fine.

❀ A strimmer makes light work of any remaining edge grass. Long-handled edging shears are useful too, but more time-consuming. Hand-held edging shears can make for slow and tiring work on larger areas of grass.

❀ If the lawn edge is ragged, neaten it with a half-moon edger, aligning it with a plank to ensure a neat, well-defined edge. For speed and ease on more extensive lawns, it may be worth hiring a powered edging machine.

PREPARING FOR TURFING AND SOWING

 !!! 45–60 MINS PER SQ M/YD ●

• **Careful preparation of the soil insures against future problems that would take both time and trouble to put right**
• **It provides the perfect surface for a lawn: the grass roots into it quickly and easily, creating a strong, vigorous lawn that will be able to withstand the wear and tear of summer traffic**

Thorough ground preparation is vital for a successful lawn, whether you are going to turf the area (*see p.38*) or grow from seed (*see p.87*). It is heavy and painstaking work, but the consolation is that it saves a good deal of time in the long term, because the care taken now helps to minimize any future problems. For larger areas, you may decide to use contractors, rather than doing the job yourself.

Clearing the site completely of weeds guarantees that the more vigorous perennials, such as dock and dandelion, which regenerate from the root and can force their way up through turf, will not make a later, unwelcome reappearance.

The initial digging opens up the soil to create good drainage, and removes any obstacles to better growth such as large stones or builders' rubble. The addition of organic matter, such as well-rotted manure or spent mushroom compost, improves the textures of both light and heavy soils because, although it seems paradoxical, it makes the soil more moisture retentive and at the same time more free draining.

There is sometimes a problem with gardens attached to brand new houses, where the builders have removed the good topsoil, leaving only poor topsoil on which grass

1 If the site is weed-infested, spray with a systemic glyphosate weedkiller which is harmless to humans and animals once dry, and leaves no residue in the soil. Clear the weeds when they have died back in 3–4 weeks' time.

2 Dig over the whole area to at least a fork's depth, clearing away any large stones or debris. Hiring a motorized rotavator or mini-plough is worthwhile for larger areas, saving a good deal of time and effort.

3 Unless the soil is well drained and obviously fertile, dig in plenty of organic matter such as well-rotted manure. This will add nutrients, open up a heavy soil, and help to bulk up lighter, sandier soils.

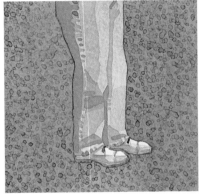

4 Rake the soil to level it, breaking up any large clods, until the surface is reasonably fine and crumbly. Now firm the soil by 'shuffle-treading' – taking very small steps with feet together – over the whole area.

TIPS

✿ If the lawn site is infested with deep-rooted weeds such as bindweed, two applications of weedkiller may be necessary, so wait for 3–4 weeks after the first spraying to see whether any new growth emerges.

✿ On heavy or waterlogged soils, or ground that is prone to waterlogging, add in plenty of grit or gravel as well as organic matter when doing the initial digging. This will open up the soil even more and improve the drainage.

✿ To save time on heavy soils, dig when they are moist but not sodden. A clay soil, for example, can be almost impossible to dig when dry and is very heavy work indeed when wet.

✿ If you need to raise the level of the ground, topsoil is the cheapest option, particularly if you buy it loose. Always check the quality (*see facing page*) and have it tipped as close to the site as possible, to save time and effort barrowing to and fro.

would struggle to grow. The only solution here is to fork over the subsoil, then buy in fresh topsoil. It is available bagged, but it is cheaper to have it delivered loose. Always examine the topsoil before it is tipped – the consistency should be something like a good loam-based compost, and it should not contain a high proportion of stones or the roots of perennial weeds.

Careful firming and levelling avoids the problems created by a bumpy lawn – the bald patches where the mower skims over a hump, for instance, and the time involved in removing the weeds that will inevitably colonize it, or the extra work of lifting the turf and re-levelling (*see p.40*).

Most gardeners are happy to level by eye, using a plank laid on the soil to indicate humps and hollows, but you can also use a system of pegs to guarantee an absolutely even surface. Mark a number of pegs at 5cm (2in) from the top, and hammer them in up to the mark, to form a grid. Lay a plank over the grid and, using a spirit level, adjust the pegs until they are exactly aligned. It is now a simple matter to even out the soil surface with a rake, until it is level with the marks on the pegs.

Raking and fertilizing guarantee the best possible start for both turf and seed, providing a comfortable environment for the roots, and feeding the grass right through to autumn. A thorough watering before laying turf or sowing helps the lawn to become established.

■ The other ideal season for preparing the ground for turfing or sowing is mid- to late autumn.

▶ *If you have a neglected, weed-infested or poorly drained lawn, it may be better to dig it up and start again from scratch.*

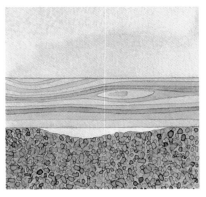

5 Place the edge of a plank over the surface of the soil, to check if it is level. If there are any humps or hollows, add or remove soil as necessary and firm it down by shuffle-treading again, until the site is completely level.

6 Rake the surface of the soil to a fine, crumbly texture, then leave it for a week or so to allow any surface weed seed to germinate. Apply weedkiller and carefully hoe or rake out the weeds when they have died back.

7 A few days before turfing, rake in a slow-release balanced fertilizer at 50g per sq m (1½oz per sq yd), spreading it evenly and raking it in lightly. This will help to feed the grass through spring and summer.

8 If the ground is dry before turfing, water it thoroughly so that the turves 'bind' easily with the soil, rooting quickly and growing on strongly and evenly. The soil should be moist to a depth of at least 10cm (4in).

LAYING TURF

  !!! 10 MINS PER SQ M/YD

- **Turfing is the easiest way to create a new lawn**
- **The laying process is simple, methodical and foolproof**
- **Turf gives instant results, transforming the garden in a matter of hours**
- **The lawn can be used as soon as the grass is growing strongly, normally within a few weeks**

Turfing is undoubtedly the easiest way to create a new lawn, and it is gratifying work because it changes the whole look of the garden in just a few hours. Growing a lawn from seed (*see p.87*) is certainly cheaper, but the grass takes longer to establish.

Your lifestyle and the extent to which you intend to use your lawn dictate the type of turf to buy, and garden centres generally stock two grades. Meadow turf contains a good proportion of coarser grasses, which can withstand a lot of wear and tear: it is ideal for families with energetic children or pets. Cultivated (seed-raised) turf has a greater proportion of fine grasses, creating a smoother finish that is suitable for average use.

It can be well worth tracking down specialist turf suppliers who stock a wider selection of grasses, from those that will withstand the pounding of a football game, to the ones that provide the fine, velvety finish that is required for bowling greens. The best suppliers grow their turf on fine mesh netting, giving the cut turf extra strength, and preventing it from stretching or breaking when laid.

The quality of the turf is crucial, because patchy, weedy or coarse turf can be very time-consuming to bring up to scratch. Inspect it when buying from the garden centre, or before it is

1 Lay turf as soon as possible after purchase. If a delay of a day or so is unavoidable, spread the turves out grass-side up on paving or on polythene sheeting in a shady position, and keep them very well watered.

2 Make sure that the ground is thoroughly saturated (*see. p.37*), then lay the first row of turves, using a paved edge or string and line as guide. Lay them without stretching, and butt the cut edges tightly together.

3 Working from a plank to avoid damaging the grass, lay the second row of turf. Stagger the line of turves in much the same way as building a wall, to minimize the gaps. Lay the remaining rows of turf in the same way.

4 Tamp down the turves with the back of a rake. This helps bind the turves with the soil, and eliminates any air pockets, so that they root down well and grow strongly. For quicker work, use a garden roller if you have one.

TIPS

❀ For very large lawns, it is worth contacting a specialist turf supplier who will deliver extra-long rolls on a wheeled laying machine, which you can buy or borrow. The turf is laid simply by wheeling the machine backwards; a 25m (80ft) row can be laid in no time at all.

❀ If just a small section of turf is needed to complete a row, place it within the row rather than at the end, where it would be much more susceptible to drying out.

❀ You may find the occasional piece of turf that is sliced rather thinly, and you will need to add extra soil or compost to raise it to the level of the surrounding turves. Similarly, you may have to remove soil to accommodate any turves that have been cut too thickly.

❀ If one edge of a newly laid lawn is exposed to hot sun, mound earth along the edge to provide protection from drying out until it is growing strongly.

off-loaded by one of the specialist suppliers. Good turf is rich green, well mown and close-knit, with sharply cut edges. The soil should be a good loam – turf grown on sandy soil can break up when handled, and a heavy clay soil can present problems later on as it is vulnerable to drying out and cracking. Check the age of the turf, too: young turf (ideally between twelve and fourteen months old) roots much more readily than older turf, which will need a great deal more watering to get it established.

Once the turf is laid, it is vital to keep it very well watered for at least 3–4 weeks and through any hot, dry weather in the first summer. You can walk on the turf immediately after laying, but keep traffic to a minimum. The grass should not be subjected to heavy wear and tear for at least two months, to allow it to concentrate its energies on rooting rather than regenerating the top-growth after any damage.

When the grass reaches about 4cm (1½in) high, begin to mow regularly. Set the blades high for the first few cuts (never less than 2.5cm/1in for a general purpose turf), gradually decreasing the height of cut over the next few weeks. Use a light mower if possible – a hover mower is ideal. Collect up the clippings for the first few weeks by using a grass box attached to the mower, or by raking them up by hand.

■ Turf can also be laid in autumn and during any mild spells through winter, provided no frost is forecast. Laying turf in summer is possible, but will involve a good deal of watering through any hot, dry spells.

▶ *Good-quality turf is essential for success when laying new lawns.*

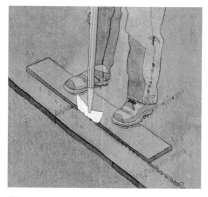

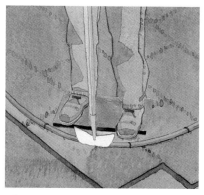

5 When laying is completed, trim away any surplus turf, using a half-moon edger and a plank as a guide. For very long edges, use string and pegs to ensure a continuous straight line, aligning the plank to the string.

6 Use a hosepipe or thick rope to outline curved edges, checking that the shape is correct by looking at it from all angles, including from house windows. Pin the pipe or rope in place, and carefully cut round it with the edger.

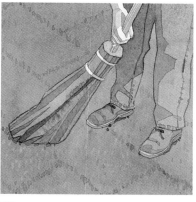

7 Scatter a top-dressing of horticultural sand mixed with compost onto the lawn, and brush it in well with a besom or broom. This will fill any small gaps between the turves, helping them to knit together and establish well.

8 Water thoroughly, so that the turves are saturated (lift one of the outer turves to check that the base is wet). Keep well watered through any dry spells, to encourage rooting and avoid shrinkage and subsequent gaps.

OVERSEEDING THE LAWN

  !! | 5 MINS PER SQ M/YD

- **Overseeding is quick work and thickens up sparse, patchy lawns within weeks**
- **It will cut down on the time involved in patching worn areas with new turf**

Areas of lawn that are subject to extra-heavy wear – relatively narrow grass paths, for example – can become very sparse and patchy. Although it might seem sensible to simply returf these areas, the problem is bound to recur. By far the best and quickest solution is to overseed. This is a technique regularly used by groundsmen to restore worn areas, turning them into a lush green carpet in just a few weeks. Areas overseeded in spring will be fully established by midsummer.

■ Overseeding can also be undertaken in autumn.

TIPS

❀ Save time and trouble in future by choosing the right type of seed. If grass is growing poorly because it is shaded, select a mix formulated for shady areas. If heavy wear is the problem, use a tough ryegrass mix.

❀ On very bald patches where the seed is more visible, it is advisable to net the area to protect it from birds.

▲ *Overseeding is the perfect technique for restoring worn grass paths.*

1 Rake the grass vigorously to roughen the soil surface, using a spring-tined rake. For ease and speed, rake when the soil is moist and more easily loosened.

2 Scatter grass seed at 35g per sq m (1oz per sq yd) and rake it into the surface. Water in, and keep well watered until the grass is growing strongly.

LEVELLING HUMPS AND HOLLOWS

 !!! | 10–15 MINS PER HUMP/HOLLOW

- **The instant way to create a smooth, even lawn**

Humps and hollows in the lawn are unsightly, and the humps can cause problems when they are scalped by the mower, leaving bald patches.

TIPS

❀ Level lawns when the soil is moist, so that the turf peels back easily without cracking or tearing.

❀ After levelling, brush a top-dressing of good soil or compost mixed with sand into the 'H' where the grass was cut, to help it to re-bind.

1 Cut out an 'H' around the hump or hollow with a spade or half-moon edger. Undercut the turf to approximately 2.5cm (1in) with a sharp spade and carefully pull it back, trying not to break or damage it.

2 Using a trowel, remove soil from a hump until the surface is level. Fill in a hollow with loam-based compost or good garden soil. Replace the turf flaps, check that the lawn is level, then firm down and water well.

NO-DIG EARLY POTATOES

  15 MINS PER 6 TUBERS

- **The no-dig method is a simple, foolproof way of growing delicious early potatoes without all the earthing up involved in traditional potato growing**
- **Once the bed is prepared, no additional digging is required**
- **Weeds are smothered by the polythene sheet**

The traditional way of growing potatoes can be very time-consuming: they are planted out in a trench and the soil must be earthed up over the foliage regularly, to ensure a good yield. When the crop is ready, it is dug up, a process which inevitably damages some of the tubers.

The no-dig method, by contrast, is simplicity itself, and is ideal for busy gardeners. Careful ground preparation, as with any crop, is vital. Potatoes need extra-fertile soil, so it is important to improve the bed by digging in plenty of organic matter, such as well-rotted manure.

Providing you ensure that the soil is moist, but not waterlogged, when the potatoes are planted (water the plot if necessary), they will need no extra maintenance except for taking measures to prevent slug damage (*see p.125*). The polythene locks in moisture, so they will need no additional watering through their relatively short growing season.

Always use fast-maturing early varieties for the no-dig method, rather than the slower maincrop potatoes. They are actually classified as 'first' and 'second' earlies, but either will do for this easy method, and they include varieties suitable for boiling, chipping, baking and salads. For ease of growth, select varieties that are certified disease resistant.

TIPS

❀ Seed potatoes (small tubers) are normally bought six weeks or so before planting time and left in shallow trays in a light, frost-free position to sprout. When planting, leave all the sprouts intact for smaller (but more) potatoes, or reduce to two or three sprouts for larger (but fewer) tubers.

❀ Always use thick black polythene to cover the bed. If the potatoes are exposed to light for any length of time, they develop green patches. These parts are poisonous, and must be cut away before cooking.

▲ *Freshly harvested, home-grown potatoes have an incomparable flavour.*

1 Lay a sheet of heavy-duty black polythene over the bed, anchoring it down by mounding soil over the edges, or tucking them down into the soil. If the planting site is in an exposed position, anchor it with wooden battens.

2 Cut crosses in the polythene sheet, approximately 30cm (1ft) apart, and bury individual potatoes 10–12cm (4–5in) deep through the holes. As the plants grow, tuck slug pellets around them to prevent damage to the new tubers.

3 The first fully open potato flowers indicate that the crop is ready to harvest (usually within 10–12 weeks) and individual plants can be harvested over the next few weeks. Cut off the top-growth close to ground level.

4 Pull back the polythene sheet to reveal the crop lying on, or close to, the surface. Harvest by hand – there will be no need to dig. Replace the polythene to exclude light from any neighbouring unharvested potatoes.

GROWING LOOSE-LEAF LETTUCE

   10 MINS PER 2M (6FT) ROW

- **Loose-leaf lettuces are long-lasting plants, reducing the need for successional sowings**
- **Individual leaves can be picked as needed**
- **Highly decorative and slower to run to seed than hearted lettuces**
- **Good pest and disease resistance**

All lettuces are easy to grow from seed, but the loose-leaf varieties are especially productive. They do not form a heart, and individual leaves can be harvested over a very long period. They are attractive plants too, with their frilled or oak-leaf foliage in all shades from bright green to deep red, and are showy enough to be grown in beds and borders as well as the kitchen garden. Grow them in a fertile, well-drained soil in a sunny position, and keep them well watered through any dry spells.
- Loose-leaf lettuces can be sown up to midsummer.

TIPS

❀ For quickest results, try the 'cut-and-come-again' method. Sow in drills 8cm (3in) apart and do not thin. When seedlings are approximately 10cm (4in) high, harvest the tops, leaving 2.5cm (1in) of stem. This will resprout, to give a second crop.

❀ Protect against slugs (*see p.125*) and keep the plot free of weeds.

▲ *Loose-leaf lettuces (here, with curly endive) have a long cropping period.*

1 Sow the seed (*see p.29*) in a well-prepared, fertile soil. When the seedlings emerge, gradually thin to 30cm (1ft), leaving a few surplus seedlings to grow on a little for use in early salads.

2 When the plants are reaching maturity, begin to harvest individual leaves as needed. If the whole head is required, leave a 2.5cm (1in) stump, which will resprout within a few weeks.

GROWING CARROTS

 ! 15 MINS PER 2M (6FT) ROW

- **Home-grown carrots have unbeatable sweetness and flavour**

Carrots grow best in a light, fertile soil in full sun. Heavy and stony soils can cause stunted, forked growth.
- Carrots can be sown in succession up to early summer.

TIPS

❀ When selecting seed, look for varieties that are resistant to carrot fly.

❀ For success on heavier soils, grow round- or stump-rooted carrots.

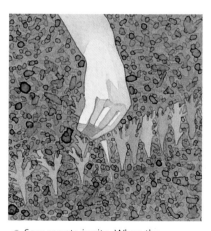

1 Sow carrots *in situ*. When the seedlings germinate, thin them to approximately 8cm (3in) apart. Remove the thinnings immediately, so that the scent does not attract carrot fly, which lays eggs on the surface. The resulting maggots cause considerable damage.

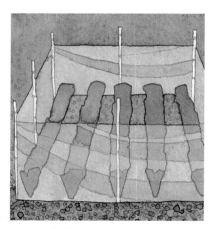

2 Take further precautionary measures against carrot fly, unless growing a variety that has some resistance. They are low-flying insects, and a 60–90cm (2–3ft) barrier of horticultural fleece or clear polythene will keep them at bay. Keep carrots well watered in dry weather.

PLANTING A RAISED VEGETABLE BED

   5–10 MINS PER SQ M/YD

• **Close planting makes maximum use of the available space**
• **The fertile, well-drained soil promotes healthy, fast-growing plants and bumper crops**

The no-dig kitchen bed is a boon to the busy gardener, because once the bed is set up, no further digging is needed. Drawing up a planting plan is a useful exercise, because it helps to clarify both the type of crops you want to grow, and the space you are likely to need for each one. If you have only a small raised bed, it makes sense to concentrate your efforts on 'premium' and fast-maturing varieties, such as sugar snap peas, French beans and spring onions. Another advantage of the no-dig bed is that the high fertility of the soil allows crops to be planted more densely than in the traditional 'vegetable row' system, so that even a small raised bed can give you surprisingly high yields.

TIPS

❀ Planting in a small blocks is both decorative and practical. A mix of crops deters insect pests – the scent of carrots, for instance, is masked if chives are planted nearby, reducing the risk of attack by carrot fly.

❀ Maximize yields by using vertical space. Trailing courgettes, melons and cucumbers can all be trained on sturdy frames, and climbing French beans take up much less ground than the dwarf varieties.

❀ Save time and trouble by selecting pest- or disease-resistant varieties when buying seed or plants – some lettuces, for instance, are much less susceptible to viruses than others.

▶ *A densely planted raised vegetable bed can produce prolific crops.*

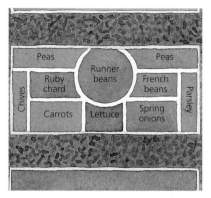

1 Once you have created the bed (*see p.113*), draw up a planting plan to make the best use of space. Site taller crops (peas and runner beans) so that they do not shade the bed. Parsley, chives and strawberries make neat, low edgings.

3 If you want to grow root crops, it is best to sow *in situ*, since they resent disturbance. Mark the sowing area with silver sand, and sow the seed in individual drills, in the same way as sowing border annuals (*see p.21*).

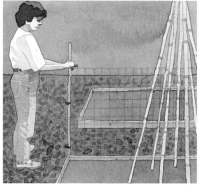

2 Working from the path, install any plant supports. For runner beans, make a wigwam of 2.5m (8ft) canes, lashed together at the top. Support peas on wide mesh plastic netting stretched between 90cm (3ft) canes.

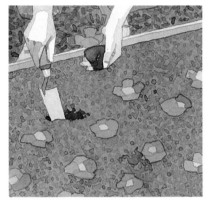

4 Set garden centre or home-raised plants in staggered rows at the recommended planting distance. These plants will eventually knit together in a dense mass, making maximum use of the bed and smothering weeds.

PROTECTING CROPS FROM LATE FROSTS

  ! ! ! 1–2 MINS PER 10 PLANTS

• **Simple protection keeps tender young crops safe from frost**
• **Protecting crops encourages more rapid growth by keeping them warm during the day**
• **it also provides protection against flying insect pests, which are especially damaging to young crops**

However warm the weather in mid-spring, there is always the danger of untimely frosts, which can wreak havoc with tender young crops. Happily, there are several simple methods of protecting plants, most of which will also promote more rapid growth by providing higher temperatures during the day. Plastic bottles, for example, act like mini-greenhouses, and horticultural fleece and polythene will also provide extra warmth.

TIPS

❀ Save time by using perforated polythene for polytunnels. It gives good ventilation, so that the sides of the tunnel do not need to be raised during the day.

❀ Covering a patch of ground with horticultural fleece or a polytunnel will warm the soil so that seed can be sown, or young plants set out, a few weeks earlier than normal.

❀ Double-walled polycarbonate sheeting, held together with cloche clips to form an A-frame, provides excellent insulation and will last for years. Where several sheets are placed together, reduce the wind-tunnel effect by sealing the ends with offcuts.

❀ 'Leaded light' glass cloches are both practical and ornamental.

▶ *A little extra protection keeps all the newly planted and seedling crops safe from untimely spring frosts.*

Protect seedlings and young plants cheaply and easily by recycling plastic soft drink bottles. Simply chop off the bottom, remove the cap and pop them over the plant to keep it warm during the day and protected at night.

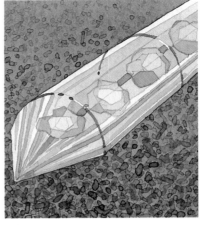

A low polytunnel can be used to protect rows of frost-tender plants such as lettuces and young peas. To prevent rot and mildew, ventilate the tunnel during the day by lifting up one side of the polythene.

Horticultural fleece, mounded with earth at the edges, gives excellent frost protection. It also protects against insect pests, and lets in plenty of light and air, so can be left *in situ* until the danger of frost has passed.

If only night frosts are forecast, cover the plants with several thicknesses of newspaper. Bury the edges or weigh them down with battens to keep the newspaper in place, and remove it during the day to allow light in.

PLANTING A HERB POT

  ! | 15–30 MINS PER POT |

• **Provides fresh, flavoursome herbs for salads and cooked dishes**
• **The pot can be sited close to the kitchen for quick and easy pickings**
• **Herbs are undemanding with excellent pest and disease resistance**
• **The flowers attract butterflies and bees to the garden**

Freshly picked herbs are delicious, and a herb pot makes a handsome addition to any garden. A mix of herbs provides good contrasts of foliage colour and form – filmy fronds of purple fennel, for example, and neat cushions of thyme. The flowers are often very attractive, and are a valuable source of nectar and pollen for butterflies and bees. They are easy, undemanding plants too, rarely succumbing to pest or disease attack, and needing very little care. Just site the pot in a sunny spot, keep watered through any dry weather, and feed once a month in summer.

TIPS

❀ Save time by using a large herb pot – the greater volume of compost means that it will need watering much less frequently than a small pot.

❀ Turn the pot around occasionally so that each plant has its fair share of sunshine.

❀ Mint spreads incredibly rapidly and swamps other plants, so save time and trouble by giving it a pot to itself.

❀ Position chives and parsley in the top of the pot to give them a deeper, moister root run.

❀ Parsley is best treated as an annual and is easy to grow from seed as long as the compost is kept moist.

▶ *A planted herb pot is both practical and very ornamental.*

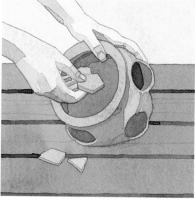

1 Water herbs, then line the base of the pot with crocks or gravel. This prevents compost from blocking the drainage hole, and also helps to provide the sharp drainage that is essential for the majority of herbs.

2 Top up with compost until it is level with the first set of planting holes. Use a loam-based compost for good drainage. Composts based on peat or peat-substitute can retain too much moisture in winter.

3 Plant the first layer by placing the herbs inside the pot and carefully easing the foliage through the planting hole. Top up with compost, firming it down to avoid any air pockets, and then plant up the second layer.

4 Top up with compost to within approximately 5cm (2in) of the rim, and plant up the top of the pot, firming plants in. Water thoroughly to settle the compost around the root balls, and place the container in a sunny position.

LATE SPRING

Late spring is a delightful time – a happy confusion of the last of the spring flowers with the first of the summer, when tulips make a brief acquaintance with early roses. There is much gardening to be undertaken, but the key thing is to prioritize, concentrating first on those tasks that will save time in the future. Feeding the lawn, for example, keeps it growing strongly, eliminating the need to weed sparse patches throughout the summer. Similarly, care taken when choosing and planting up bedding plants ensures that they grow well, providing a mass of summer colour.

▲ *The sweet fresh scent of lily-of-the-valley* (Convallaria) *fills the air in late spring.*

PRUNING SPRING-FLOWERING DECIDUOUS SHRUBS

 !! 10–15 MINS PER SHRUB

• **A simple two-step pruning method for a number of popular spring-flowering shrubs**
• **Pruning maximizes the annual display by encouraging plenty of new growth that will bear more, and better, flowers**

Shrubs that flower on the previous year's new stems can begin to look untidy and top-heavy if left unpruned. The plant becomes congested with old, unproductive wood, there is little new growth from the base and the flowers are produced only on the newest, topmost stems. Pruning keeps plants compact and shapely, stimulates new growth that will bear next year's blooms and removes unsightly dead flowers. Spring shrubs that should be pruned after flowering include flowering currant (*Ribes*), forsythia, kerria and the spring-flowering forms of spiraea and tamarix.

■ Use the same pruning method for philadelphus, weigela, deutzia and exochorda after they have flowered in summer.

TIPS

❀ Prune shrubs very lightly in their formative years, taking out only the flowered stems. Full pruning can be undertaken once they have reached their mature height and spread.

❀ Prune as soon as possible after flowering. This gives plants the maximum time to produce the new wood that will ripen over the summer and bear next year's flowers.

❀ While pruning, shape up the plant by cutting back awkwardly placed, crossing stems and any twiggy growth.

❀ Annual pruning is advisable for shrubs that flower on last year's new stems, but they will stay in fairly good shape if left unpruned for a year or two.

❀ For speed and ease when pruning woodier shrubs, such as forsythia and tamarix, use loppers on the larger stems. Long-handled loppers make for quick work on tall specimens.

❀ To encourage vigorous new growth, water thoroughly after pruning, feed with a balanced fertilizer, and apply a mulch to conserve moisture.

1 Prune out a few of the older main stems to open up the shrub (here, flowering currant) and to encourage vigorous new growth from the base.

2 Cut back flowered stems just above a bud or sideshoot, slanting the cut away from it. The ensuing growth will bear next year's flowers.

SELECTING BEDDING PLANTS

  5 MINS PER 10 PLANTS

- **Checking plants over before buying saves all the time and trouble involved in nursing sickly specimens back to health**
- **Selecting well-grown plants, at just the right stage for planting, guarantees easier, more colourful summer displays**

One of the keys to easy summer displays is to choose bedding plants that are at their peak of fitness. Those that have received any kind of check in growth will be much more difficult to look after, taking time and trouble to get back into shape. The turnover in plants at garden centres is very rapid at this time of year, so if there are only poor specimens of a variety that you need, just wait for a day or two rather than compromising on quality.

TIPS

❀ Succulent-leaved plants, such as geraniums (*Pelargonium*), rarely show signs of wilting, even when unwatered for days. Lift the pot to check for dryness – it will feel much lighter than a well-watered pot.

❀ Plants grown in strips are tempting because they are relatively cheap, but root damage is inevitable when splitting them up, and they will take longer to get established.

❀ Set plants in a warm, light position indoors until you are ready to plant them up. Keep the soil moist.

❀ If buying early, or if planting is delayed, regularly inspect the plant's root system. If it is becoming congested, transfer the plant to a larger pot so that it does not suffer a check in growth.

▶ *Tobacco plants* (Nicotiana) *produce a profusion of flowers for months on end.*

1 Select a plant with sturdily compact growth, bright, vibrant leaves and no sign of pests or diseases. When selecting a flowering plant, check in the crown · to see that there are plenty of new buds as a guarantee of future flowers.

2 Inspect the base of the pot. Reject any plants with a mass of congested roots around the drainage holes in favour of those with just a few roots emerging, which are at just the right stage for planting up.

❀ Reject any plants that are leggy or yellowed. Leggy plants have not been kept in enough light, and yellowing is an indication that they are suffering from lack of food and have probably been on sale for some time.

❀ Avoid wilting plants. They may have been allowed to dry out several times, and any check in growth can be very debilitating. Although the plants will revive when watered, it is unlikely that they will ever fully recover.

PLANTING OUT BEDDING PLANTS

  ! 10 MINS PER SQ M/YD ▶

- **Bedding plants can be used to create spectacular displays**
- **They provide months of colour in exchange for a little extra effort**
- **Bedding is the ideal temporary infill for new beds of permanent plants, providing colour and interest, and keeping down weeds**

Bedding plants are inevitably time-consuming, but they are invaluable for spectacular summer displays, and can also be used to fill ground in new beds until more permanent plants have matured. Geraniums (*Pelargonium*), with their lovely colours and forms, will tolerate both poor soil and dry conditions. They are also very easy to overwinter (*see pp.24 and 86*). To keep bedding plants looking their best and in full flower production, regularly remove spent blooms.

TIPS

❀ If the soil is poor, dig in organic matter before planting, or apply a balanced fertilizer.

❀ Set plants in staggered rows, spacing them according to their eventual spread. They will bush out to make a dense, even cover that looks good and smothers annual weeds.

❀ Keep bedding plants well watered through any dry spells in the first 3–4 weeks until they are growing strongly. Thereafter, water only if they show signs of flagging, or if there is a prolonged period of drought.

❀ Tobacco plants (*Nicotiana*), pansies (*Viola*), brachycomes, begonias, busy lizzies (*Impatiens*) and fuchsias are easy, showy plants for partial shade.

▶ *Free-flowering and compact, busy lizzies (*Impatiens*) are ideal bedding plants for bright colour in a shady spot.*

1 Plant after the last frosts in your area. Dig over the soil if it is compacted and rake to a fine, crumbly texture. Water the plants about one hour before planting, to help the roots 'bind' with the soil.

2 Remove the plant from the pot and tease out any roots that are circling the root ball. If left as they are, they will continue growing in circles, rather than spreading out and down in the soil.

3 Using a trowel, make a hole large enough for the root ball. Set the plant in so the root ball is just slightly lower than the surrounding soil. Fill in, firming the soil around the root ball.

4 Make a slight saucer-shaped depression around the plant, so that the top of the root ball is flush with the soil. This helps catch and hold water, channelling it to the roots. Water well.

POND PLANTING

  !! 10 MINS PER PLANT

- Pond plants provide year-round colour and interest, using a mix of evergreen and flowering varieties
- They need little additional care after planting, and have excellent pest and disease resistance
- The floating leaves of waterlilies provide shade which discourages the growth of algae

The advent of warmer weather makes this the ideal time to plant up a pool or pond. There is an enormous range to choose from, with waterlilies (*Nymphaea*) at the top of the list. These lovely plants are essential in a sunny pool, both for their exotic flowers and for the sculpted leaves, which shade the water and discourage the growth of unsightly 'pea soup' and blanketweed algae. Oxygenating plants, such as parrot's feather (*Myriophyllum aquaticum*), are vital too for the health of both the water and the pondlife.

TIPS

❀ Check over plants before buying, looking for any signs of snails or their jelly-like eggs, blanketweed and for tiny floating plantlets of duckweed, which can be highly invasive.

❀ To make planting quicker and easier, use a fine mesh crate which does not need to be lined.

❀ Ordinary garden soil can be used when planting, provided it is loamy and has not recently been treated with manure or fertilizer. Proprietary potting composts are unsuitable, since they contain fertilizer, which will encourage a build-up of algae.

❀ Always set plants at the recommended depth, which is the distance between the top of the pot and the surface of the water.

▲ A well-stocked pond with a good mix of plants is a delight and will be equally attractive to wildlife.

1 Choose a planting crate that will easily accommodate the plant's roots and line with hessian.

2 Part fill the crate with moist, loamy soil or proprietary aquatic compost and set the plant (here, iris) in the centre, firming it down gently.

3 Top up with more soil or compost to within 2.5cm (1in) of the rim, firming it down around the plant so that it is securely anchored in position.

4 Cover the surface of the crate with a 1cm (½in) layer of gravel or pea shingle to prevent the soil from washing away when it is set in the water.

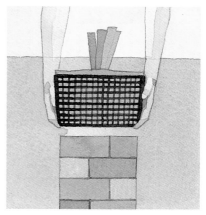
5 Carefully lower the crate into the pond at the recommended planting depth. Bricks or blocks can be used to adjust the height.

PROPAGATING POND PLANTS

   10 MINS PER PLANT

• **Division is an easy way to increase stock of favourite plants**
• **Propagation cuts costs, particularly of more expensive pond plants such as waterlilies**
• **It improves the appearance of rhizomatous plants, such as irises, removing old, unproductive material**

Water gardening is the ideal pastime for the busy gardener, since aquatic plants are tough and trouble-free for the most part, and there is no weeding and certainly no watering to do. Once planted, they can be left to their own devices, apart from a quick annual tidy-up in autumn (*see p.95*). Propagating by division is a fast and easy way to increase your stock of aquatic plants, and cuts the cost of water gardening dramatically since some plants can be extremely expensive. Lifting and dividing can also be necessary in order to reduce the spread of a plant that has outgrown its position, or to rejuvenate a 'stand' of iris. These grow outwards on the rhizomatous rootstock, and the centre of the plant becomes woody and unproductive.

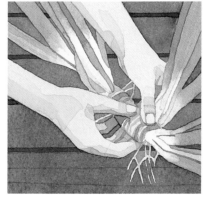

1 For rhizomatous plants (here, iris), split or cut them apart into manageable pieces, each with healthy leaves and plenty of roots.

2 Trim the leaves, but not so severely that the cut surface will be submerged. Trim up the base, and cut back the roots by half.

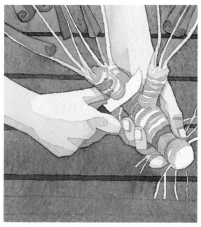

To divide waterlilies, remove a 'branch' from the rootstock, using a sharp knife. Plant up by inserting the branch vertically.

Fibrous-rooted plants (here, *Carex*) can be divided by hand. If the roots are very congested, lever them apart with two forks placed back to back.

TIPS

❀ Save time by selecting non-invasive plants. The dwarf reedmace (*Typha minima*), for example, is just as attractive as the greater reedmace (*T. latifolia*) but much less vigorous, growing on neatly for many years before division is necessary.

❀ The roots of some water plants are so densely entwined that they are virtually impossible to divide in the normal way. It is much quicker and easier to divide them up with a sharp pruning saw. Provided each portion has its fair share of roots and top-growth, it should grow well.

❀ Oxygenating plants are easily propagated from cuttings. Simply snip off 15cm (6in) lengths, tie them in small bundles, and plant these in a large planting crate. Watermint (*Mentha aquatica*) also grows well from cuttings, which should be inserted singly.

❀ It is also possible to propagate water plants by sowing fresh seed (dried seed does not remain viable). Water forget-me-not (*Myosotis scorpioides*) is especially easy. Just shake the flowered plant over a pot of compost. Cover the seed lightly with more compost and keep saturated.

▲ *Waterlilies* (Nymphaea) *are magnificent pond plants, and easy to propagate.*

TAKING SOFTWOOD CUTTINGS

| 15 MINS PER POT |

• **Softwood cuttings are quick and easy, taking advantage of the vigour of spring growth**
• **It is a good way to increase stocks of favourite plants, or to ensure successors for varieties that are not reliably long-lived**

Taking softwood cuttings is a good way to propagate a wide range of hardy perennials and shrubs, including philadelphus, fuchsia and deciduous forms of cotoneaster and viburnum. Climbers such as wisteria and honeysuckle (*Lonicera*) can also be propagated by this method. The vigour of the sappy spring growth means that the cuttings will root remarkably quickly and can be potted on before they are planted out in autumn. Taking softwood cuttings is an especially good way to propagate plants that have a tendency to be short-lived, such as perovskia and shrubby lavateras.

TIPS

❀ Take cuttings in the early morning when the plants are at their freshest. It is vital that cuttings do not wilt before being potted up.

❀ The easiest way to prevent your cuttings from drying out, particularly if several are being taken, is to seal them inside a polythene bag so that they stay fresh. Keep the bag shaded.

❀ Excess moisture can cause rot, so if condensation forms, wipe the propagator lid and open the vents, or remove the polythene bag for a while.

❀ Clematis cuttings require a slightly different method. Trim the cutting just above a leaf joint, leaving a 2.5–5cm (1–2in) length of stem below it. Remove one of the leaves and insert the stem in the compost.

1 Take 10–15cm (4–6in) cuttings from vigorous shoots (here, hydrangea). Reject damaged shoots and any that are in flower or are forming flower buds.

2 Using a sharp knife, trim off the lower leaves and make a straight cut just below a leaf joint, reducing the cutting to approximately 8–10cm (3–4in) long.

3 Insert the cuttings around the edge of a pot of cuttings compost to half their length, spacing them so that the leaves are not touching.

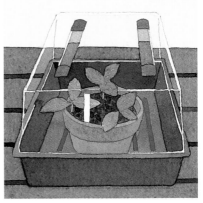

4 Water moderately and place in a heated propagator in a well-lit but not sunny position. Water as necessary, ventilating if moisture builds up.

5 When the cuttings are well rooted (tug them gently, or inspect the base of the pot for any emerging roots), divide them up and pot them on individually.

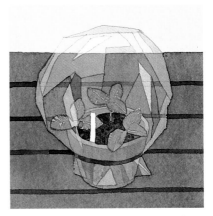

✿ The pot can also be sealed inside a plastic bag. Inflate the bag before securing it, to keep it away from the leaves, and stand in a warm, light spot.

PLANTING POTS, TUBS AND WINDOW BOXES

 ! | 5–15 MINS PER POT | ◖

- **Planting pots is quick and easy, providing superb summer displays of colourful bedding plants**
- **Just one or two interestingly-planted containers can create striking focal points**
- **Water-retaining crystals and slow-release fertilizer help cut down on watering and feeding**

Summer container displays are by no means essential, but if you have a little extra time to care for them, they can be absolutely stunning. Most summer bedding plants have a very long flowering period, blooming from early summer right through to mid-autumn or even later in a mild year. Terracotta pots are simple to plant up, and plastic pots are even easier, requiring no extra drainage. Large tubs need a good drainage layer (which also saves on compost), and window boxes will benefit from a layer of crocks or gravel.

TIPS

✿ Save time on watering by adding water-retaining crystals to the compost. When wetted, they swell to form mini-reservoirs and can cut watering by a third or more. Lining the inside (but not the base) of terracotta pots with polythene will also help to reduce moisture loss.

✿ Cut out feeding altogether by mixing a slow-release fertilizer with the compost at planting to feed plants all season long.

✿ For easy one-step watering, leave a good gap between the top of the compost and the rim of the container, to retain the water until it is absorbed by the compost.

▶ *Pots of different shapes and sizes look especially good clustered together in a sunny corner of the garden or patio.*

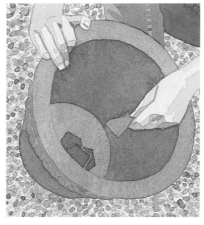

1 Plant up containers after the last frosts. If using a terracotta pot, line the base with crocks to aid drainage. To save weight on balconies or roof gardens, use broken-up polystyrene.

2 Fill the pot with compost to within approximately 5cm (2in) of the rim and firm it down. Use a multi-purpose compost – decanted compost from growbags can be a cost-effective option.

3 Water the plants well an hour or so before planting, then set them out on top of the compost, swapping them around to obtain the best possible combination of colour and form.

4 Using a trowel to make planting holes, set the plants in at the same level as they were in their pots, firming them in. Water thoroughly and top up any hollows that may appear.

PLANTING A HANGING BASKET

  30–40 MINS PER BASKET

• **The all-round planting technique produces spectacular displays**
• **Moss is much more attractive than artificial liners, especially in the early stages**

A mossed wire basket needs a little extra care in planting and watering, but repays the effort by bushing out into a spectacular, full display. Hanging 'pot' baskets may be easier (especially the self-watering types), but never have quite the same impact because planting is confined to the top of the pot. The use of moss, rather than an artificial liner, provides an attractive, natural background for the plants in the early stages. After planting, keep the basket in a warm, well-lit position indoors to grow on. Hang it outdoors after the last frosts, and keep evenly watered – a high-low pulley or an angled hose-end lance (*see p.62*) will help to make this easier. If you have several baskets that are grouped together, it may be worth considering installing an automatic watering system (*see p.70*) to do the work for you. If going on holiday, take measures to keep basket plants growing well (*see p.77*).

1 Water plants, then sit the basket on a large pot to steady it. Line the lower half with a tightly packed 2.5cm (1in) layer of sphagnum moss and place polythene in the base to help retain moisture.

2 Top up with compost to the level of the moss. Add water-retaining crystals and slow-release fertilizer and mix in, to help retain moisture and keep plants well fed. Firm the compost down.

3 Water plants well. Remove a plant from its pot and ease the foliage through the wires. Set in the remaining side plants at about 15cm (6in) intervals.

4 Line to the top of the basket with moss and top up with compost; firm down. Add the remaining plants, fill any gaps with compost and water well.

TIPS

❀ To prevent damage to bushy-headed plants when planting the side of the basket, carefully roll a tube of newspaper around the foliage. Pass the tube through the wire and remove.

❀ Artificial basket liners make for easy work, but can look rather stark until the plants have bushed out.

❀ For effective watering, make a thick wall of moss at the top of the basket. This holds in water and prevents compost from washing away. Using

loam-based rather than multi-purpose compost also aids water retention.

❀ For ultra-quick planting, use just three or four plants of vigorous, bushy trailers such as Surfinia petunia, which can grow to 90cm (3ft) or more.

❀ Larger baskets can be very heavy, so always hang on a well-secured bracket.

❀ Turn baskets occasionally so that plants have their fair share of sun and do not become leggy or yellowed.

▲ *A well-planted hanging basket bushes out into a great globe of colour.*

PLANTING FLOWER TOWERS AND POUCHES

   20–30 MINS PER TOWER/POUCH

• **Flower towers and pouches are a colourful way to decorate walls, fences and pergolas with a host of summer bedding plants**
• **They are quick and easy to plant up and very cost-effective, lasting for several seasons**
• **They retain moisture well, cutting the frequency of watering**

Flower towers and pouches are relatively new, and very easy to plant up and maintain, the closed environment providing good water retention. Towers create a cascade of colour, whether hung against a wall or suspended from a pergola for all-round viewing. Pouches are used as 'living plaques', ideal for brightening a dull stretch of wall or fence, or for setting beside a doorway. You can vary the effect of towers and pouches by your choice of plants. Compact varieties such as busy lizzies (*Impatiens*) and semperflorens begonias create a neatly symmetrical shape, packed with small flowers – and both, incidentally, will thrive in partial shade. Bushier plants, such as bidens and petunias, are ideal for more informal planting. The water-retaining qualities of towers and pouches make them less suitable for winter plantings.

1 To plant a tower, fill the base of the tower with compost to the level of the first planting holes and firm it down. Cut a cross in the plastic where indicated and ease the plant in so that the root ball rests on the compost.

2 Repeat the procedure for the next two layers, then fill to the rim with more compost, water well and hang the tower on a strong bracket. If it is to be hung at a low level, you can also plant the top of the tower.

1 To plant a pouch, fill the pouch with compost, firming it down as you go. Take care that the corners at the base are well filled or the compost could sink when the pouch is hung up. Push open the pre-cut slits, ready for planting.

2 Water the plants well, then set them in, firming compost around the root balls. Stand the pouch up to plant the top. Water well, then place the pouch flat to grow on for 2–3 weeks before hanging it up.

TIPS

❀ Water flower towers by topping up the reservoir at the base of the tower. Water pouches from the top – a hose-end lance makes for easier watering (*see p.62*).

❀ As with other container plantings, use slow-release fertilizer and water-retaining crystals to feed plants and cut down on watering.

❀ For ultra-quick planting, use vigorous, bushy trailers such as bidens, trailing petunia and ivy-leaved geraniums (*Pelargonium*), using no more than six plants per tower or pouch.

❀ If planting up early, place the tower or pouch in a warm, bright position indoors to grow on, hanging them out when all danger of frost has passed.

▲ *Use pouches to enliven dull walls.*

FEEDING THE LAWN

  | 15 MINS PER 5 SQ M/YD |

• **Feeding gives instant results, greening up the grass within days**
• **It encourages denser growth which suppresses weeds and moss**
• **It strengthens the grass and keeps it healthy**

Feeding the lawn may seem counter-productive, making it grow faster so that it needs mowing more often. In fact it helps to save time in the long run, encouraging thicker growth that smothers weeds and moss, both of which can take time and trouble to eradicate. This dense growth also makes it less susceptible to drying out in a summer drought. It makes the whole garden look considerably better, turning a tired, yellowing lawn to a vibrant green within a matter of just two or three days.

■ If the lawn is looking jaded by mid-autumn, feed it again to toughen it up for winter, using a specially formulated autumn feed.

TIPS

❀ Use a feed formulated for spring/summer, which encourages lush, rapid growth.

❀ Some spring/summer fertilizers also contain weed- and moss-killer, saving time and effort by dealing with three problems at once.

❀ Spread granular fertilizer when rain is forecast, saving the trouble of watering the fertilizer in dry weather to prevent it from scorching the grass.

❀ Feeding the lawn is not a routine task. If the grass is growing strongly and is a healthy green, then you should simply leave it alone.

▶ *A lush, well-fed lawn glows with health and makes the perfect backdrop for flower-filled borders and planters.*

❀ For even distribution of granular fertilizer, make a 1 sq m/sq yd bamboo frame. Weigh out the correct amount of fertilizer then divide in half, scattering the second half at right angles to the first.

❀ Using a calibrated lawn spreader is another good way to feed the lawn. Weigh out the amount of fertilizer needed for the whole area, divide in half and make two runs, one lengthways and the other crossways.

❀ A special hose-end spray gun fitted with a fertilizer dispenser makes quick work of feeding the lawn. Simply insert a lawn fertilizer block into the dispenser, set to the correct concentration, and spray.

❀ Apply liquid fertilizer by using a can with a dribble bar attachment. Use a large can to avoid having to refill several times, mixing the fertilizer with water at the recommended rate and applying evenly.

SUMMER

EARLY SUMMER

Sunny days in early summer make gardening a real pleasure, with every excuse for plenty of rest periods to enjoy the scent and colour of a whole host of plants bursting into flower including, of course, the first great flush of roses. Most of the work at this time is simply a matter of ensuring good displays throughout summer – dead-heading roses, for instance, and pruning early-flowering clematis. Container plantings of summer bedding will also need routine care, to keep them in flower right through to the first frosts.

▲ *Plants such as achillea and delphiniums provide a mass of colour in early summer.*

DEAD-HEADING ROSES

  !!! 5–10 MINS PER PLANT

• **Dead-heading is a quick and easy way to encourage a succession of blooms from repeat- or continuous-flowering roses**
• **It helps to keep plants shapely, well balanced and looking their best**

Dead-heading is an essential job in the summer months for the vast majority of roses that either flower continuously or have a single main flush in early summer followed by a further scattering of flowers. If the first blooms are left to seed, the plant assumes that its task (producing the next generation) is done and no further flowers are necessary. The only roses that do not need dead-heading are those once-flowering shrub roses – such as *Rosa moyesii* and the grey/green-leaved *Rosa glauca* – that are valued for their colourful hips that persist through autumn and into winter. Whilst dead-heading, the gardener is also able to enjoy the sight and scent of the remaining blooms and the clusters of the new buds promising more beautiful flowers to come. It is an easy task, with a pleasing monotony to it, and the rewards are great.

TIPS

❀ Dead-heading also shapes up the plant, so use your best judgement when deciding where to cut – a long, straggly stem, for instance, can be cut back quite hard.

❀ For guaranteed new blooms, always cut back to flower-bearing wood – i.e. beyond the leaves that bear only three leaflets rather than the usual five.

❀ Dead-head individual blooms of cluster-flowered roses, then cut back the whole truss when all the flowers on the stem have faded.

❀ Feeding roses in midsummer (*see p.65*) will also help to ensure continuity of bloom.

❀ Roses occasionally produce 'blind' shoots with no sign of buds at the tip. Cut back this unproductive growth by at least half.

❀ Save time when dead-heading climbing and rambling roses by spreading a cloth or polythene sheet around the plant to catch the faded blooms. This makes it very easy to transfer them to the compost heap.

To remove faded flowers, use secateurs to cut back to just above an outward-facing bud or leaf joint. Angle the cut to slope away from the bud.

The bud will now be stimulated to form a new flower-bearing stem. This will face outwards and keep the bush open and well balanced.

PRUNING EARLY LARGE-FLOWERED CLEMATIS

   !! | 10–20 MINS PER PLANT

• **Pruning early large-flowered clematis after flowering is an easy way to encourage later blooms**
• **The training in of new shoots keeps plants well groomed and provides good wall cover**

The early-flowering clematis, appearing in late spring and early summer, are much prized for their enormous blooms and free-flowering habit. Mauve-pink 'Nelly Moser' and blue-purple 'The President' are among the best known of this popular group. They produce their flowers on the previous year's growth, and will often produce a second, smaller crop of early autumn blooms on the new shoots formed in spring and summer of the current year. Pruning them after flowering helps to maximize the autumn display and keeps plants neat and shapely. Feed, water and mulch after pruning to encourage vigorous new growth.

▲ *The showy blooms of C. 'Nelly Moser'.*

1 Immediately after flowering, cut out approximately one-third of the older, woodier stems to within 30cm (1ft) or so of the base.

2 In late summer or early autumn, train the new growths onto the framework, tying them in loosely with soft twine.

PRUNING EARLY SPECIES CLEMATIS

  !! | 10–20 MINS PER PLANT

• **Pruning keeps vigorous plants under control**

The small-flowered species clematis, flowering from winter to late spring, include the vigorous *Clematis montana* and evergreen *C. armandii*. Pruning after flowering promotes new flowering wood.

TIP

✿ Two of the daintiest spring clematis are *Clematis alpina* and *C. macropetala*, 2.5m (8ft) high, which can be left unpruned for 2–3 years.

1 First thin out any stems that are very congested to let in light and air, cutting them right back to the framework of the plant. Then remove any twiggy or damaged growth to improve the overall appearance of the plant.

2 Prune back all flowered stems to within one or two buds of the main branches, and cut back any stems that are outgrowing the allotted space. Tie in any untrained stems to provide a good, even foliage cover.

CONSERVING WATER

  !!! 5–30 MINS PER TASK ◑

- **Careful use of water saves money if water is metered**
- **It makes the most of rainwater, recycles domestic water and keeps plants watered without waste**

Conserving water makes good sense both ecologically, and even more financially in households with water meters. So take advantage of the water-saving methods outlined here (*and see also pp.65 and 71*). The simplest way to conserve water is to concentrate your efforts on the most vulnerable plants – young vegetables, for instance, and anything recently planted. Hand watering or using a soaker hose is much more efficient than a sprinkler, which waters all plants regardless of their needs. A water butt can be used to store up to 250 litres (75 gallons) of rainwater, and domestic water can be recycled – water from the bath or sink is fine to use on established plants. Growing drought-resistant plants is another easy way to cut down on water use, because once established, they need no extra watering at all. Many grasses and herbs, as well as a wide variety of silver-leaved border plants, will thrive in poor dry soil in a sunny spot.

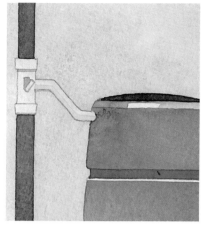

Collect rainwater in a butt. Fitting a diverter to a drainpipe will help fill it even more quickly. In hard water areas, rainwater is especially useful for watering lime-hating plants such as azaleas and rhododendrons.

Hose-end guns are much more efficient than all-over sprinklers, which water indiscriminately. They deliver water exactly where it is needed, in just the right quantity. Adjustable guns (from jet to spray) are the most useful.

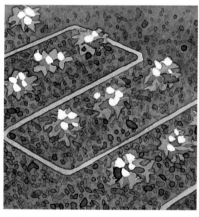

Use a soaker or seep hose for effective watering of young vegetables and bedding plants. Snaked around the bed, it gently leaks water to 30cm (1ft) deep and 40cm (16in) wide.

A soaker hose is even more efficient if buried or covered with mulch, because less water is lost through surface evaporation. The coarse texture of chipped bark helps lock in moisture.

TIPS

❀ Take time to save time by watering thoroughly. A light watering is actually counter-productive because it just encourages roots to the surface, where they will perish in the next dry spell.

❀ Save time and trouble by fitting a diverter to collect household water, rather than carrying it out to the garden in cans and buckets. Fitted to the drainpipe of baths and sinks, it has an on/off switching mechanism so that

water is easily diverted into a hose. This can be fed into a water butt for cooling and storage, or used directly on the garden if already cool.

❀ Use hose-end appliances that have an end-stop, to conserve the water that would otherwise be wasted when going to turn off the tap.

❀ Mulching (*see p.17*) helps to conserve a good deal of moisture.

▲ *A water butt helps to cut back on the use of domestic water in the garden.*

DIVIDING SPRING BULBS

  !! 20–30 MINS PER CLUMP

• **Division rejuvenates overcrowded bulbs, bringing them back to their full flowering potential**

• **It increases spring displays by creating two or three groups of bulbs from a single original clump**

• **It makes the most of offset bulbs, giving them the space required to mature and flower**

• **Keeps bulbs healthy by eliminating any diseased specimens**

Established groups of bulbs can deteriorate with age. As more and more bulbs mature, they become congested, each one fighting for its fair share of nutrients and water, and flowering diminishes. Lifting and dividing rejuvenates them, and creates two or three more well-flowering clumps, for extra spring colour. To provide an effortless transition to the new planting site, lift the bulbs while they are dormant – floppy, yellowing leaves are a good indication that root growth has ceased. Bulbs that are still in active growth can receive a severe check if lifted and replanted.

TIPS

❀ Poor flowering can also be caused by not removing spent blooms, or by under-feeding. So when bulbs start to fail, try dead-heading and feeding initially (*see p.31*), before going to the extra trouble of lifting and dividing.

❀ When replanting, space mature bulbs approximately twice their own width apart, with smaller offset bulbs between them. Closer planting is counter-productive, since they become overcrowded all the sooner, needing further attention.

▶ *Spring-flowering Narcissus 'Thalia' can be divided in early summer.*

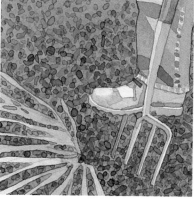

1 When the leaves are beginning to die back, use a garden fork to lift the whole clump, digging carefully around and under it in order to avoid spearing any bulbs. For easier digging, choose a time when the soil is moist.

2 Separate out the clump by hand, breaking it first into small groups, then into individual bulbs (here, *Narcissus*), retaining any small offset bulbs. Handle the bulbs carefully, to avoid causing any damage.

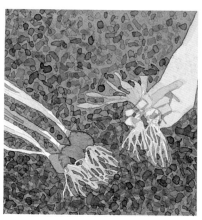

3 Check over the bulbs very carefully, looking for any signs of disease or damage. Discard any that are marked, pitted, holed, or showing signs of rot, so that only healthy plants are replanted.

4 Replant the bulbs in well-prepared ground. Use a trowel or bulb planter (*see p.84*) to make planting holes, and set the bulbs in at their original depth, using the white portion of stem as a guide.

SUMMER CARE OF CONTAINER PLANTS

   5 MINS PER CONTAINER

- **Regular watering and dead-heading maximizes displays**
- **Mulching saves time by reducing water loss from pots and tubs**
- **Easier basket watering with hose-end lances and high-low pulleys**

Summer container plants are, without a doubt, time-consuming, but regular care pays dividends, keeping them healthy and vigorous. Neglected plants are much more vulnerable to pest and disease attack, which take time and trouble to remedy later. Dead-heading is an easy task that keeps plants tidy and prevents them from setting seed and fading away. Regular watering is, of course, essential, particularly in hot, dry conditions, and if you find that it is simply taking up too much time, the answer is to install a watering system (*see p.70*). Mulching pots and tubs helps to conserve moisture, while cocoa-shell and gravel mulches will also deter slugs and snails.

TIPS

❀ If slow-release fertilizer was not added to the compost when planting up, feed plants weekly with a high-potash fertilizer.

❀ In hot weather, water in the cool of the morning or evening, to reduce moisture loss by evaporation.

❀ The easiest way to re-wet a hanging basket is to soak it in a large bucket of water for half an hour or so.

❀ Planted pots look good clustered together in a group, and in a sunny position this provides a little extra shade so that the compost does not dry out quite so quickly.

▶ *Geraniums* (Pelargonium) *flower very freely if regularly dead-headed.*

🌸 Dead-head bedding plants regularly, to prevent them from diverting their energy into setting seed. Snap the faded flower off cleanly close to the main stem, to avoid leaving an unsightly stalk.

🌸 To save the time and effort of using steps and a watering can to keep baskets well watered, invest in a hose-end lance. Specially designed for baskets, it delivers a fine, penetrating spray.

🌸 A high-low pulley attachment also makes for easy basket watering. Pull the basket down to a convenient height for watering, then push to send it back into position.

🌸 Mulch pots to reduce water loss by evaporation. Cocoa-shell and gravel are ideal for bedding plants, while pebbles make a decorative mulch for specimen plants.

PLANTING UP TOMATOES IN A GROWBAG

  ! 20 MINS PER GROWBAG

• **Using a growbag is an easy way to grow tomatoes and a wide range of other plants**

• **The compost inside a growbag provides a sterile environment, with no risk of soil-borne pests and diseases**

• **Can be tucked into any sunny corner, making best use of all available space**

Growbags are tremendously useful – instant containers that can just be popped down in any sunny spot and planted up very quickly. They provide excellent growing conditions, as the nutritious compost is free of all pests and diseases, and the plastic keeps the roots warm for fast, vigorous growth. Tomatoes are one of the most popular growbag crops, and the cordon types are the easiest and neatest to grow, fruiting on a single main stem. Bush tomatoes have a sprawling habit and are much more prone to attack from slugs and snails. Keep tomatoes evenly watered, especially when the fruit is ripening, feed once a week when the first pea-sized fruits appear, and pinch out the top of the main stem when four or five trusses have set.

Other crops that are suitable for growbags include lettuce, peppers, aubergines and French beans – just check the recommended spacing and make planting holes accordingly. They can also be used for courgettes and outdoor cucumbers which, being vigorous plants, are best planted two per bag. A good crop of strawberries, too, can be raised in a growbag. Feed leafy and podded crops with a nitrogenous fertilizer, and fruiting crops, such as strawberries and peppers, with a high-potash feed.

TIPS

❀ Growbags are also useful for growing summer bedding plants. Make individual planting holes, and grade the heights, using bushy trailing plants to disguise the front and sides of the bag.

❀ For easy, effective watering, make a few drainage slits near the base of the growbag. When water runs from these, it is safe to assume that the compost is well watered.

❀ At the end of the growing season, recycle growbag compost by spreading it on the garden or adding it to the compost heap.

▲ *Provided they are regularly watered and fed, prolific crops of tangy tomatoes can be raised in growbags.*

1 Cut three crosses in the plastic to make planting holes, tucking in the flaps. For easy watering, mound the soil between the flaps to create a slight dip that catches and channels the water.

2 Water the tomato plants an hour or so before planting, and make planting holes in the compost. Remove the pots and set the plants in, firming the compost around the root balls. Water well.

3 For a free-standing growbag, use special growbag supports, inserting 1.5m (5ft) canes through the holding rings. Tie the plants in as they grow, removing all sideshoots.

If you want to hide the plastic, plant annual trailers, such as lobelia or bidens, with the crops. Water before planting, gently separate strip plants and set in front of the tomatoes.

MIDSUMMER

High summer is a time for relaxing and enjoying the garden at its very finest. Border displays are reaching their peak, bedding plants are in full flower, and the air is full of heady scents from dawn to dusk. Happily, then, there are no arduous tasks at this time of year. Just a quick cut-back of hardy perennials to encourage a second flush of flower, a little extra care for the lawn through hot, dry spells, a few simple measures to keep pools looking good, and the pleasant work of taking cuttings and harvesting herbs.

▲ Long-flowering campanulas are ideal plants for a sunny border.

CUTTING BACK HARDY PERENNIALS

  !! | 5 MINS PER CLUMP |

• **An easy task that instantly improves the look of plants by removing unsightly faded flowers**
• **Cutting back maximizes flowering potential by encouraging the production of a second flush of flowers**

Cutting back the faded flowers of hardy perennials is quick and easy work that serves two purposes. It keeps plants tidy, and encourages a second, smaller flush. Some, such as lupins and delphiniums, are cut right back; others – campanulas and phloxes, for example – are cut back gradually.

❀ Using secateurs, cut back faded flower spikes (here, lupin) to ground level. This tidies the plant and, by preventing it from setting seed, will often induce a second, smaller flush of flowers.

❀ Many plants produce a large central truss of flowers, with further flowers on sideshoots. Cut out the central truss (here, campanula) as it fades, to maximize the flowering potential of the sideshoots.

TIPS

❀ Shear alchemillas (lady's mantle) and hardy geraniums to ground level after flowering, to produce neat clumps of fresh leaves and, often, a further scattering of flowers.

❀ Cutting back prevents vigorous self-seeders, such as columbines (*Aquilegia*), from setting seed.

▶ A little judicious cutting back helps to maximize the colour from border plants throughout the summer.

SUMMER ROSE FEEDING

  !!! 2 MINS PER PLANT

• **Feeding encourages more flowers**

Feeding roses in midsummer is a quick and easy task that gives them the boost they need for further blooms right through to autumn. Once-flowering roses, too, will benefit from a summer feed.

TIPS

✺ Lightly rake in granular fertilizers.

✺ Apply foliar feeds on an overcast day, to reduce the risk of sun scorch.

🌼 After the first flush of flower, feed roses with a proprietary rose fertilizer. Sprinkle granular fertilizer around the plant at the recommended rate, keeping it away from stems or leaves.

🌼 In times of drought, spraying plants with a foliar feed is more effective. This bypasses the roots, which cannot take up the nutrients in granular feeds without moisture in the soil.

KEEPING VULNERABLE PLANTS WELL WATERED

  !!! 5–30 MINS PER PLANT

• **Applying a mulch saves time spent watering and weeding**
• **Mulches provide good insulation**

New plants, especially when planted against a wall, can dry out very quickly in hot summer weather. Getting water directly to the root ball, and mulching, will help them to establish well.

TIPS

✺ Water plants thoroughly an hour or so before planting, as well as afterwards. It is much more difficult to wet a root ball after planting and plants will struggle.

✺ A soaker or seep hose (*see p.60*) is the easiest and most effective method to keep newly planted beds and borders well watered through any hot dry spells, as it gently leaks water where it is needed.

▲ *A cool, moist root run is essential for all clematis – here, 'Ernest Markham'.*

🌼 For accurate watering of newly planted shrubs and perennials, sink a pot into the ground beside the plant. When topped up, this will gently seep water directly to the plant's roots.

🌼 Plants on house walls are especially vulnerable to drying out. An ornamental mulch of pebbles or cobbles, laid when the soil is moist, prevents loss of water by evaporation.

🌼 Laying landscape fabric, through which rain can permeate, is another good way to conserve moisture and eliminate weeds. Disguise it with a layer of bark chips or gravel.

SUPPORTING AND TRAINING CLIMBERS

 !!! 1 HOUR MAX FOR ALL TASKS ●

• Careful training makes the most of climbers, providing an attractive even cover and avoiding ugly bunching and overcrowding
• Using young, sappy growth which is pliable and easy to guide into position makes for quick work
• Horizontal training encourages maximum flower from both climbing and rambling roses

Many wall-grown climbers need support, and subsequent training gives a good even cover that maximizes their impact. Galvanized wire is useful for a wide range of climbers, but it can sag under the weight of heavier plants such as wisteria unless stretched very taut. Trellis is more decorative and can be mounted so that it is removable for wall maintenance. For durability, choose trellis that has been pressure-treated with preservative. Tying in all new growths keeps plants looking good. Use plastic-covered wire ties rather than twine, which will rot.

TIPS

❁ To allow for wall maintenance, secure trellis to the battens with hooks and eyes rather than screws. The plant and trellis can be gently removed from the wall when necessary.

❁ Plastic mesh makes a practical support for comparatively lightweight climbers, such as the smaller varieties of clematis, and annuals such as sweet peas (*Lathyrus*).

❁ Self-clinging climbers, such as ivy (*Hedera*) and climbing hydrangea (*Hydrangea anomala* subsp. *petiolaris*), need no wall support but can be trained in, using individual vine eyes.

▶ *Regular training (here, a climbing hydrangea) creates superb displays.*

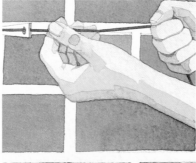

The simplest way to support climbers is with galvanized wire stretched between vine eyes. Keep the wire as taut as possible, especially if it is to support heavier, woody climbers.

Tie in new growths regularly, spacing them to produce a good even cover of foliage and flower. Loosely twist rather than knot the tie so that it does not bite into the stem as it grows.

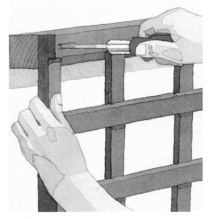

Fix trellis to 5cm (2in) thick battens, rather than directly onto the wall, using galvanized screws. This creates a gap between the wall and the plant so that air can circulate more freely.

Train climbing and rambling roses horizontally in order to stimulate the maximum number of flowering sideshoots. Tie them in while the stems are still young and whippy.

SUMMER POOL CARE

  !! | 20 MINS PER SMALL POOL |

- Dead-heading keeps pools looking neat and eliminates the need to weed out young plants of vigorous self-seeders
- The removal of blanketweed and duckweed, and the planting of waterlilies to discourage 'pea soup' algae, keeps pools clear
- Thinning out untidy, congested oxygenating plants improves the appearance of the pool

Summer care of the garden pool takes only a few minutes at a time but can make a substantial difference to its appearance. Flowering plants need just a quick dead-heading to prevent them from setting seed, and overcrowded oxygenators can rapidly be thinned by hand or with a rake. Algae and filamentous blanketweed can be a nuisance, and are almost inevitable in any pool, but they are simple to remove and there are several ways to deter their regrowth.

TIPS

❀ For quick and easy removal of the tiny floating plants known as duckweed, scoop them out with a long-handled net.

❀ To deter the growth of algae and blanketweed in sunny spots, grow plenty of waterlilies to shade the water: a ratio of one-third leaf to two-thirds water surface is ideal. Oxygenating plants will also help by robbing the algae and blanketweed of the minerals they need.

❀ Chemical treatments for algae and blanketweed should be used with the utmost care as incorrect doses can cause an unhealthy pool.

▶ *Waterlilies* (Nymphaea) *are not only beautiful, but they also deter algae.*

❀ Cut out faded flower stems to keep plants neat and to avoid the chore of weeding out young plants of vigorous self-seeders such as iris.

❀ If oxygenating plants, such as *Elodea*, are crowding the surface, thin them out with a rake, or lift the basket and trim them back.

❀ Blanketweed can also be raked out, but it is much easier simply to insert a stick and twist it so that the blanketweed wraps round it.

❀ Fish can become distressed by lack of oxygen in very hot or thundery weather. Aerate the water with a hose-end spray or by turning on a fountain.

DEALING WITH SUCKERS

 !!! 5–10 MINS PER PLANT

• **Removing suckers prevents them from taking over on grafted plants, saving the time and trouble of digging out and replanting**
• **It eliminates the untidy thicket of suckering growth at the base of some trees and shrubs**

Suckering stems do just what the name suggests – suck vitality from the plant on which they are produced. Grafted plants are particularly vulnerable; many roses, for example, are grown on wild rootstocks, from which vigorous suckers can arise. If left, they weaken the plant and may eventually take over. Plants that are top-grafted onto a clear stem can also produce suckers at any point between the roots and top-growth. Some plants produce suckers from their own roots, either as part of their natural habit or in response to damage to the roots or top-growth. If a plant is continually producing suckers it may be easier, in the long term, to dispose of it.

TIPS

❀ Suckers of grafted plants are usually easy to identify, with a noticeable difference in stem and leaf colour and form.

❀ Correct planting of roses (*see p.102*) helps prevent suckering.

❀ Take care when hoeing or planting around shallow-rooted trees and shrubs, to avoid damage which could encourage suckering.

❀ Remove any suckers that form at the edges of pruning cuts on trees and shrubs.

▶ *Ornamental cherries, such as* Prunus serrula, *can produce a thicket of suckers at the base of the trunk.*

1 To remove a rose sucker, which is produced from the roots of grafted plants, trace it to its point of origin by carefully scraping away soil.

2 Using a stout glove for protection, tear the sucker away from the rootstock (cutting it encourages regrowth). Replace the soil and firm it down.

Prune out suckers at, or near, the base of trees (here, *Prunus*), trimming as close as possible to the point of origin. Suckers in the surrounding area can be cut or pulled out.

Pare off any suckers on the stems of top-grafted trees and shrubs (here, a standard rose) and rub out any subsequent regrowth. Pulling off stem suckers can damage the bark.

TAKING SEMI-RIPE CUTTINGS

 ! 15 MINS PER POT

- **Semi-ripe cuttings are a simple and inexpensive way to increase stocks of a wide range of popular shrubs and climbers**
- **The use of a propagator guarantees quicker rooting**

Taking semi-ripe cuttings is a reliable and easy method to propagate a vast range of woody plants, including roses, honeysuckle (*Lonicera*), lavender, viburnum and holly (*Ilex*). It is also a good way to perpetuate short-lived shrubs such as lavatera and perovskia. Semi-ripe cuttings root well in warm summer temperatures, but a heated propagator gives even faster results. Once rooted, pot the cuttings individually and place in a cool, well-lit place indoors, out of direct sun. Keep them moderately watered in winter and plant out in spring.

- Semi-ripe cuttings can be taken between mid- and late summer.

TIPS

❀ To reduce moisture loss from larger plants, cut them in half.

❀ For good air circulation, position cuttings so that leaves do not overlap, and ventilate the propagator if moisture builds up.

❀ For speed when taking a lot of cuttings, insert them directly into a compost-filled propagator.

▲ *Cuttings of choisya root easily.*

1 Select a non-flowering sideshoot that is just starting to go woody at the base. Trim the cutting (here, choisya) below a leaf joint to 10–15cm (4–6in), retaining some of the woodier material.

2 Dip the cut base in hormone rooting powder and insert approximately 5cm (2in) deep at the edge of a pot of cuttings compost. When the pot is full, water and place in a heated propagator.

CUTTINGS IN WATER

 ! 1 MIN PER CUTTING

- **The easiest propagation method of all, and no special equipment**

Many plants will root in water, from geraniums (*Pelargonium*) to willows (*Salix*) and ivies (*Hedera*). It is such a quick and simple method that it is well worth trying with any plant.

TIPS

❀ This method can also be used to root many houseplants.

❀ Once rooted and potted up, treat as semi-ripe cuttings (*see above*).

1 Take cuttings 10–15cm (4–6in) long, making a clean cut just below a leaf joint. Trim off the lower leaves and place in a clear glass jar to monitor root progress. Top up the water as needed, changing it if cloudy.

2 When a good root system has formed on a cutting, remove it from the water and line a 9cm (3½in) pot with cuttings compost. Spread the roots over the compost, fill in and firm down. Water well to settle the roots.

INSTALLING A PATIO WATERING SYSTEM

   1 HOUR PER MINI KIT ●

- **Provides efficient patio watering at the turn of a tap**
- **Ensures economical watering, so that not a drop is wasted**
- **Computerized systems solve the problem of holiday watering**

Patio plants can need twice-daily watering in the hottest weather, but this time-consuming work can be eliminated altogether with a patio watering system. Available in kit form or as separate items, these can be tailored to fit any site, using wall clips and adaptors. They save water too, supplying it just where it is needed, in the right quantity – an important consideration for metered households. They can also solve the problem of summer holiday watering with the addition of a water computer. This can be programmed to deliver water for a specific period, several times a day. Some suppliers also offer a moisture sensor that overrides the computer, to ensure that the containers are not over-watered in rainy spells.

TIPS

❀ For ultra-efficient watering, use adjustable rather than fixed delivery drippers. These can be regulated so that individual containers receive just the right amount of water.

❀ To remove any impurities, which could clog up the tubes, occasionally remove the end sleeve that caps the supply tube and flush water through the system.

❀ Watering systems are equally effective in beds and borders and in the vegetable garden.

▶ *A patio watering system keeps pots evenly moist without waste, especially if adjustable drippers are used.*

1 Attach the pressure regulator to a threaded outside tap, ensuring that it is firmly in position, before connecting the main supply tube.

2 Thread the main supply tube around the patio, securing it with wall clips. Cut the tube and use elbow connectors for right-angle bends.

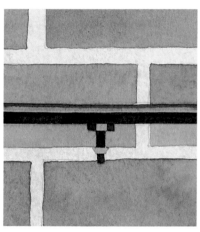

3 To run the narrower micro tube to individual containers, make a hole in the main supply tube with the punch provided, siting it as close as possible to the container. Insert a micro tube adapter.

4 Attach the micro tube, cut to the desired length and fit with an adjustable dripper. Suspend this over the container using a micro-tube stake to hold it firmly in place.

LAWN DROUGHT CARE

  5 MINS MAX PER TASK

- **A little extra care helps to keep the lawn looking good through even a prolonged drought**
- **Mowing higher than normal traps dew and smothers weeds**
- **Thorough watering is efficient and can actually save water**
- **Leaving grass clippings on the lawn provides a little extra moisture**

The lawn is such an important garden feature that it is well worth the little extra effort needed to keep it looking good through a drought. Cutting the lawn higher than normal is a simple measure that creates a dense, bushy sward which traps dew and smothers weeds. Watering with a sprinkler is easy too, but it is vital that you water very thoroughly, at fortnightly intervals. Watering little and often is counter-productive, encouraging roots to the surface, where they perish in the next dry spell. Leaving the grass clippings to decompose helps to provide extra water and nutrients. A mulching/recycler mower shreds them extra-fine, and can be used all year round to eliminate the work involved in collecting clippings.

TIPS

When adjusting the mower blades, raise the height of cut according to the type of grass: to 2.5cm (1in) for fine lawns, 4cm (1½in) for general purpose, and 5cm (2in) for heavy-duty lawns.

If you are concerned about water conservation, you can either use recycled water (see p.60), or leave the lawn unwatered. It will look parched, but will eventually recover.

▶ *A thorough sprinkling greens up dry, yellowed grass within days.*

Raise the mower blades – the top of the lawn will still look neat and even, but longer grass traps more dew and channels it to the roots.

To sprinkle the lawn effectively, mark a straight-sided jar at 10cm (4in). Place in the line of spray, turning off when the level is reached.

Remove the grass box from the mower in times of drought. The clippings, which are composed of 90% water, will supply a little extra moisture, provide nutrients, and help to trap dew.

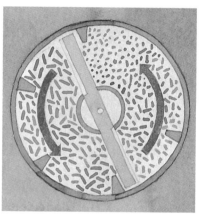

For finer clippings that decompose even faster, use a mulching mower. Special 'kickers' at the edge of the drum keep the clippings airborne for several cuts, shredding them extra-fine.

PROTECTING CROPS FROM PESTS

  !!! 15 MINS PER CROP

- **These simple pest control methods are easy to install**
- **They avoid the use of chemicals, which take time to apply and can harm beneficial insects**

Flying insect pests and their larvae can be very damaging to carefully nurtured crops. Birds, too, can be a problem, stealing soft fruit as it ripens. But the simple expedient of draping crops with horticultural fleece, or protecting with netting, will keep them all at bay.

TIPS

❀ Inspect crops carefully before netting them and deal with any existing pests. Once the crop is covered, pest damage may go unnoticed for some time.

❀ Always make sure you secure the edges of fruit netting. Birds tend to creep under an unsecured net and, apart from damaging the crop, they may become trapped inside.

▲ *The caterpillars of the large white butterfly can devastate cabbage crops.*

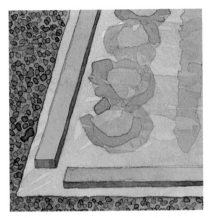

❀ Cover the crops with horticultural fleece to protect them from flying insect pests without loss of light, air or water. Secure it with battens.

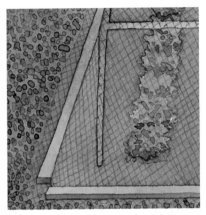

❀ Protect soft fruit (here, strawberries) from bird attack by covering it with 2.5cm (1in) mesh netting. Drape it over the crop, or stretch it over a frame.

PRUNING APPLE AND PEAR TREES

 !!! 30 MINS PER SMALL TREE

- **Summer pruning opens out the tree to let in sun and air**
- **It stimulates fruit production**

The summer pruning of vigorous apple and pear trees prevents over-crowding, stimulates the production of fruiting wood and stops them from outgrowing the allotted space.

TIP

❀ Drastic pruning can shock the tree, so spread the job out over a number of weeks.

❀ Apple and pear trees can produce a forest of vigorous new shoots by midsummer. These crowd the tree, depriving the centre of light and air, and divert energy from fruit production.

❀ Using secateurs, cut these new shoots back to within 3–4 leaves to encourage the formation of fruiting wood at the base. Extra-vigorous upright shoots can be pruned out altogether.

HARVESTING HERBS

 ! 10 MINS PER BUNCH

- **Drying and freezing are quick and easy ways to ensure plentiful supplies of herbs for winter use**
- **Fast processing maximizes flavour**
- **Dried herbs are viable for up to a year, frozen herbs for six months**

Many herbs die back in autumn, but by drying or freezing them you can continue to enjoy their flavour through the winter. Pick only the best, freshest material and process as quickly as possible to preserve the volatile oils. Pack freezer herbs immediately, and hang drying herbs in a warm position with good air circulation – for maximum flavour they should, ideally, be dried and stored within one to two days. As well as storing dried herbs individually, you can make up your own mixes – a tarragon- and thyme-based mix for chicken dishes, for example. Frozen herbs will last for six months, and dried herbs will keep their flavour for up to a year.

TIPS

❀ Carefully inspect harvested herbs for any dirt or pests, but do not wash since this will delay the drying process.

❀ For fast drying, microwave fresh herbs on full power, checking every half minute until crisp.

❀ Many herbs can be either frozen or dried, but there are exceptions. Parsley, coriander and tarragon, for example, are best frozen, while sage, thyme, kitchen bay leaves and rosemary should be stored dried.

❀ To harvest seed such as caraway, hang whole stems and secure a paper bag loosely over the seedheads.

▶ *A well-stocked herb garden provides rich pickings for drying and freezing.*

1 To harvest herbs for drying, choose a dry, sunny morning and pick whole stems. Tie in small bunches and hang in a warm, airy position indoors.

2 When the leaves are thoroughly dry and brittle, strip them off the stalks onto a clean sheet of paper, crumbling them up into small pieces.

3 Tip the herbs into a dark glass jar, seal and store in a cool, dry place away from sun. If using a clear glass jar, store in a dark cupboard.

Alternatively, pick herbs as step 1, pack fresh into freezer bags in small quantities, seal, label and freeze. The leaves crumble easily when frozen.

LATE SUMMER

The garden seems to pause in late summer, as if in preparation for the wind-down to autumn. Borders are still full of bright colour, but it gradually starts to taper away, and trees can become heavy and listless in dry weather. Temperatures begin to decrease too, making any essential tasks much easier to accomplish. Priorities now include pruning wisteria and rambling roses, routine maintenance of walls and fences, holiday care of containers and the planting of strawberries for luscious crops next year.

▲ *Glowing gold and crimson are two of the predominant colours of late summer.*

WISTERIA TRAINING AND PRUNING (1)

  !!! 30 MINS PER 3M (10FT) PLANT

• **Formative training creates a cascade of colour from well-spaced, attractively displayed flowers**
• **Twice-yearly pruning encourages maximum flowers**

Wisteria, with its great waterfalls of late spring and early summer blossom, is one of the most desirable of all climbers. The initial training and twice-yearly pruning are admittedly time-consuming, but essential for successful flowering.

■ For the second, late winter, stage of training and pruning *see p.117.*

To display the flowers to their best advantage, train wisteria against a wall on wires 45cm (18in) apart (*see p.66*). To create the basic framework, tie in sideshoots horizontally, leaving a single stem to grow upwards.

Begin the two-step pruning regime by shortening sideshoots on the main framework to within 4–6 leaf joints. Leave well-placed outermost shoots to grow on, if necessary, to extend the framework.

TIPS

❀ For guaranteed good flowering, buy the more expensive grafted wisteria rather than seed-raised plants.

❀ Water well after pruning, and keep watered through dry spells in late summer, when next year's flower buds are forming.

❀ For easier pruning, grow plants as staked standards in half-barrels to constrict their growth.

▶ *Careful pruning in late summer and late winter guarantees a tumbling cascade of flowers from wisterias.*

PRUNING RAMBLING ROSES

 !!! 20–30 MINS PER PLANT

- Hard pruning removes older, less productive wood
- It encourages the production of vigorous new flowering stems from the base of the plant
- It keeps plants shapely and restricts them to the allotted space

Rambling roses (with just a couple of exceptions) bloom only once, but their free-flowering habit creates spectacular displays that can last for several weeks. The long, whippy stems are easy to train, making them ideal for covering arches and pergolas as well as walls; they can also be left to scramble at will through trees and large shrubs. Rambling roses flower best on stems produced the previous year. The pruning regime, apart from tidying the plant and easing any congestion, promotes the growth of these new stems by removing some of the older wood.

TIPS

✿ In the first two or three years after planting, prune only to remove weak or diseased growth, and cut back healthy sideshoots by 8–10cm (3–4in).

✿ Use your best judgement when cutting out stems from the base, removing only one or two if the plant has not produced a good number of replacement stems.

✿ For easy collection of prunings, place a large polythene sheet on the ground under the plant.

✿ Although annual pruning of rambling roses is advisable, it is not essential. They will continue to flower well, and can be left for two or three years before the build-up of old, unproductive stems become unsightly.

▶ Rosa 'Félicité Perpétue' is a very free-flowering, semi-evergreen rambling rose.

1 After flowering, use loppers to cut out up to one-third of the oldest, woodiest stems at ground level. This encourages the production of vigorous new stems from the base, which will flower profusely the following season.

2 Cut back any unflowered sideshoots on the remaining stems to within two to four leaves of the main stem, to promote good flowering the following year. Cut back any lateral growth that has outgrown the allotted space.

3 Prune out any flowered sideshoots to keep the plant looking tidy, taking them back to within approximately 2.5cm (1in) of the main stem, so that no more than two leaves remain.

4 Tie in all new growths from the base with plastic-coated wire ties, twisting rather than knotting them so that they do not damage the stem as it grows. Train stems horizontally to promote flowering.

FENCE AND WALL MAINTENANCE

  !!! 1 HOUR PER STRUCTURE ●

• **Regular maintenance saves the trouble and expense of replacement**
• **Simple measures that extend the life of garden structures can also enhance their appearance**

Taking a little time to maintain garden structures saves both time and money in the long run, avoiding the upheaval and expense of replacing them. Well-maintained fences and walls, for instance, will last almost indefinitely. For wooden structures, water-based preservative is the most pleasant to use and the least harmful to plants. Do your best to keep plants out of the way while applying it, although a few splashes will do no lasting damage. Preservatives are available in a wide range of colours, and can be used to smarten up all kinds of garden structures from sheds to wooden obelisks. The mortar in garden walls can deteriorate with age, but repointing it is a relatively quick and easy task, particularly if you use a proprietary mix.

TIPS

❀ For effective treatment of wooden structures, apply preservative when the wood is thoroughly dry.

❀ Avoid using creosote wood preservative, which is poisonous to both plants and humans, cannot be used on fences that support climbers, and has an unpleasant smell.

❀ Smartening up painted walls is fast and easy work. Simply brush off any loose paint with a wire brush and apply fresh paint suitable for exterior brickwork. If the bricks are in poor condition, weatherproof them with a chemical sealant before painting.

▶ *Coloured wood preservative can transform the humble garden shed.*

All wooden structures benefit from a weatherproofing coat of preservative every three or four years. Water-based preservatives are the least harmful to plants and are available in a great variety of colours.

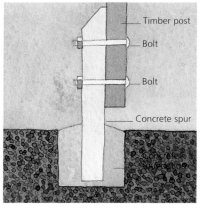

To repair a wooden fence post that has rotted at the base, first excavate the soil around it, then saw off the rotten portion and treat the cut with preservative. Bolt a concrete spur to the post and concrete it in.

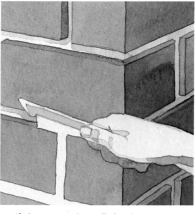

1 If the mortar in walls begins to crumble, repointing will be necessary. First, scrape out all the old loose mortar to a depth of approximately 2.5cm (1in). with an angle-bladed paving weeder.

2 Moisten the joints, then pack the mortar in with a trowel, pressing it down firmly. Finish with a chamfered edge that is slightly indented at the top and flush with the bricks at the bottom.

HOLIDAY CARE OF CONTAINERS

  !!! 10–30 MINS ALL TASKS ◐

- **A few simple tasks can keep container plantings in good condition during holiday absences**
- **These measures provide for the plants' watering and health needs**
- **Care is especially important for expensive specimen plants**

Container plantings can suffer greatly if left untended for long periods, and some plants may not recover. Keeping them going while you are on holiday can be a problem, but happily there are several ways round this. The obvious answer is to ask a neighbour to water them for you, but if this is not possible, absences of up to a week can be covered by setting them in shade and watering well. For absences of one or two weeks, a home-made capillary watering system (*see right*) will keep them evenly moist. Dead-heading plants, and checking them over for pests or diseases before you go, will also help to keep them productive and healthy while you are away.

TIPS

❀ If containers are too large to move, mulch them with gravel, pebbles or chipped bark, to slow down moisture loss by evaporation.

❀ Check the efficiency of capillary watering a few days before going away. Larger pots may need two or even three strips to keep them moist.

❀ Keep small pots moist by setting them in a box lined with damp compost and tucking moist newspaper around them.

❀ Automatic watering systems (*see p.70*) are a boon at holiday time.

▶ *Densely planted baskets are very vulnerable to drying out.*

To prevent bedding plants from setting seed, dead-head thoroughly shortly before going away. At the same time, treat any pest or disease attack that could debilitate plants, by removing affected material or spraying.

Cluster containers together in a shady position sheltered from wind, to minimize moisture loss. Support hanging baskets by placing in buckets or large pots. Just before going away, water thoroughly.

1 To keep containers moist during a 1–2 week absence, set up a simple capillary watering system. Stand a large bucket on bricks so that it is above the level of the containers and fill with water.

2 Cut capillary matting into 4cm (1½in) strips. Cluster the pots, and place one end of each strip in the base of the bucket, and the other end deep in the compost of each container.

MAXIMIZING THE CROP

  !! 5–15 MINS PER TASK

- **Promote bumper yields of repeat-cropping vegetables and keep plants growing strongly and evenly by undertaking several simple tasks**
- **Regular picking provides the tastiest, tenderest vegetables**

Home-grown crops are so delicious that any measures to prolong the cropping period are time well spent. One of the simplest ways of keeping many vegetables in full production is simply by picking them regularly to induce further flowering and cropping. Peas, beans, cucumbers, marrows, courgettes, peppers and aubergines will all benefit from this treatment, and it provides regular supplies of the youngest, most exquisite vegetables. Watering is important too, and is especially critical at the flowering stage – flowers will fail if the plant is too dry, reducing the overall yield. Mulching after watering reduces the amount of additional watering needed, and will also add some nutrients to the soil. It is especially beneficial for raspberries, which are very shallow-rooted. Feeding helps to prolong the life of greedy crops such as runner beans and courgettes.

Pick repeat-cropping vegetables regularly (here, French beans) to prolong the cropping period and increase the overall yield. If left unpicked, they will cease to flower.

To help with the pollination of runner beans, especially in cool spells when there are fewer insects about, mist plants to encourage the distribution of pollen.

To prevent flower drop in dry conditions, water crops well (here, autumn-fruiting raspberries), then apply a thick mulch of organic matter to help lock in moisture.

To help extend the growing and cropping period, give plants a boost with a high-potash fertilizer. For the quickest results, use a foliar feed, spraying it onto the leaves.

TIPS

✽ Pick podded crops when they are young, before the seed begins to cause bulges in the pods.

✽ Watering in liquid fertilizer will also feed plants, but it should be applied when the soil is already moist. On a dry soil, the nutrients are locked in until it rains, or until the plant is well watered.

✽ It makes good sense to collect seed for next year's crops. Leave a few last pea and bean pods to mature on the

plant. When the pods have yellowed, shell them and spread the seed on trays until dry and hard. Store in paper bags in a cool, dry place until ready to sow.

✽ To mulch plants, use good organic matter such as well-rotted manure, spent mushroom compost or home-made compost. As well as locking in moisture, mulches keep roots cooler through any prolonged hot spells and save the gardener a good deal of time by suppressing the growth of weeds.

▲ *Feeding, mulching and spraying encourages bumper crops of beans.*

PLANTING STRAWBERRIES

  15 MINS PER
6 PLANTS

- **Home-grown, freshly picked strawberries have superb flavour**
- **Autumn planting should ensure excellent yields next year**
- **Strawberries are easy to care for**
- **A mix of varieties guarantees a longer cropping period**

Home-grown strawberries are delicious, and they produce excellent crops in their first year after an autumn planting. Good ground preparation is essential for success, but once planted, strawberries need very little aftercare. The main requirement is watering during any dry spells after planting, and again after flowering. Individual plants will last for two or three seasons before they begin to lose vigour. When this happens, buy in fresh stocks and plant them in a new bed – they are very susceptible to viruses, which persist in the soil. Strawberries can also be grown successfully in pots, tubs and growbags.

TIPS

❀ Extend cropping by growing a mix of early, mid- and late summer strawberries, together with perpetual-fruiting varieties which produce a few good fruits in summer and crop more heavily in autumn.

❀ To keep plants healthy and pest-free, clean them up after cropping by removing the older leaves and any straw and weeds.

❀ Alpine strawberries, with their tiny, intensely aromatic fruits, make excellent ground-cover plants for beds and borders in sun or partial shade. The yield is small, but they can be used to mix with 'standard' strawberries to add flavour.

▶ *Strawberries crop particularly heavily in their first year.*

1 Choose a sunny planting site and dig over, incorporating plenty of well-rotted manure or compost. Just before planting, scatter a balanced fertilizer at 90g per sq m (3oz per sq yd) and lightly fork it in.

2 Mark out slightly mounded rows 75cm (30in) apart and space the plants 45cm (18in) apart. Set them in with the crown at ground level, spreading out the roots. Fill in, firm down and water well.

3 When the fruits begin to form next summer, protect them from soil-splash by laying strawberry mats or by tucking straw under and between the plants. As fruits ripen, protect against slugs (*see p.125*).

The juvenile plants that form on long-running stems can be removed, or used to create fresh stocks. Peg them down to encourage rooting, and once growing strongly, sever the stem, lift and transplant.

AUTUMN

EARLY AUTUMN

Early autumn signals a shift of atmosphere in the garden, with that indefinable, prickly scent which conjures up images of misty mornings and fallen leaves. Summer borders may be on the wane, but there is still much to enjoy, particularly if you have planted a good range of late-flowerers such as chrysanthemums and heleniums. A major priority for this time of the year is the planting of spring bulbs in borders and pots, for extra colour next year. Other seasonal tasks include the creation of lawns from seed, potting up herbs for winter pickings and planting cabbages for nutritious spring crops.

▲ *The bright berries of* Cotoneaster *'Cornubia' enliven the autumn garden.*

BORDER CLEAR-UP

  !!! 45 MINS PER SMALL GARDEN

• A few quick tasks keep the garden looking good through autumn
• Removing visual clutter makes the most of remaining flowering plants
• Forking over improves soil health by opening up compacted ground, letting in rain and air

As the glories of summer fade, the garden can start to look a little neglected, but a quick clear-up of the borders will soon have it back in shape. Hardy perennials that are past their best can be tidied up simply by removing the faded flower stems, leaving a neat rosette of foliage. The visual clutter of plant supports that have served their purpose can be collected up in a trice, together with any unsightly plant debris – two easy tasks that will make a surprising difference to the overall look of the garden. Forking over any compacted soil provides the finishing touch, making a pleasing background for plants still in flower.

TIPS

❀ A flush of weeds can appear after cutting plants back, especially if the weather is warm, so keep the hoe close at hand – dispatching them at the seedling stage will save a lot of work later on.

❀ Knock soil off canes and stakes and store them, ready for the winter wash- and brush-up (*see p.121*).

❀ Keeping paved areas free of litter also makes a great difference to the overall look of the garden, so make a clean sweep of paths and patios.

Using secateurs, cut back faded flowers of hardy perennials (here, achillea). This keeps them looking neat, and highlights other garden plants that are still in full flower.

Remove any redundant canes and other plant supports from beds and borders, and clear up twiggy or leafy debris – a large capacity refuse bag makes a handy receptacle.

Finally, lightly fork over any bare soil to a depth of no more than 5cm (2in), taking care not to disturb shallow-rooted plants. This opens it up to rain and air, and gives a tidy finish.

PLANTING A CONTAINER-GROWN SHRUB

  !!! 20 MINS PER SHRUB

• **Careful planting saves time in the long run, by creating strong, sturdy plants that are much less prone to pest and disease attack**

• **Mulching after planting conserves moisture and keeps down the weeds that colonize freshly dug ground**

Container-grown shrubs can be planted throughout the year, but autumn is the optimum time. The soil is still warm, encouraging rapid root establishment for vigorous new top-growth next year, and autumn rains will cut down on the need for watering. Careful planting involves a fair amount of work, but is well worth it for these invaluable plants that are the backbone of any garden – both as ornamental plants in their own right, and as a good backdrop for other perennials and annuals. It also ensures smooth, even growth, creating a healthy plant that is much less susceptible to pests and diseases, which can be extremely troublesome to eradicate.

TIPS

❀ Save time and trouble by choosing a shrub that is suitable for your soil. Rhododendrons, for instance, need acid, peaty conditions, and trying to grow them on any other soil is a thankless task.

❀ Check the shrub's ultimate spread and plant accordingly to save the trouble of having to move it later.

❀ Improve the drainage of clay soils by adding plenty of gravel or pea shingle to the soil mix before filling in the planting hole.

❀ It is important to keep newly planted shrubs well watered through any dry spells in autumn and during their first summer.

1 Water the plant thoroughly before planting. Dig a hole approximately twice the width of the root ball, forking over the sides and the base. Mix the excavated soil with organic matter.

2 Remove the plant from the pot and tease out any congested or circling roots. This encourages them to colonize the surrounding soil, so that the plant becomes established much more quickly.

3 Set the plant in, checking that the top of the root ball is level with the surrounding soil. Adjust the level, if necessary, by removing or adding soil.

4 Fill in around the root ball with the soil mix, firming down each spadeful. This ensures that there are no air pockets where roots would perish.

5 Once the hole is full, firm the soil down with your heel. This is especially important in exposed sites, to protect taller shrubs from wind-rock. Water well.

6 Surround the shrub with a mulch such as bark chips. This locks in moisture, insulates the roots against winter cold and smothers weeds.

PLANTING BULBS IN BEDS AND LAWNS

  !!! 15 MINS PER CLUMP

• **Bulbs are easy and dependable for delightful spring displays**
• **Careful bulb planting ensures larger, more colourful displays from year to year**

Spring bulbs (a blanket term that includes corms and tubers) provide invaluable colour in the garden from late winter to early summer. They are robust, easy plants and will live on almost indefinitely if carefully planted. The trick is to give them plenty of room to establish and produce offsets that will provide even more flowers in the future. For the most effective displays, plant in largish clumps of between eight and ten bulbs. The bulbs will, eventually, become overcrowded and need dividing (*see p.61*), but this takes many years with well-planted bulbs. Most bulbs prefer a sunny position, but daffodils, hyacinths, bluebells and snowdrops will all flower well in partial shade.

■ Delay planting tulips until mid- to late autumn. To establish well, they should be planted at least three times their own depth in full sun.

TIPS

❀ Choose firm, plump bulbs with no sign of damage or mould. 'Double-nosed' bulbs are the best value, producing the most flowers.

❀ Save effort by waiting until the soil is moist before digging planting holes. Hard ground makes hard work.

❀ Bulbs such as crocus look very pretty in the lawn. For easy planting, undercut and peel back the turf, set in the bulbs, replace the turf, firm, and water thoroughly. For maximum impact, plant in single-colour groups.

▲ *Crocus flowers open out like stars when placed in full sun.*

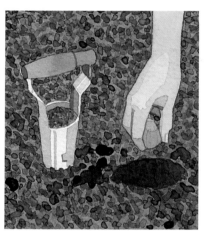

1 A bulb planter is ideal for group plantings on light soils. Simply push it into the recommended depth and pull out a plug of soil.

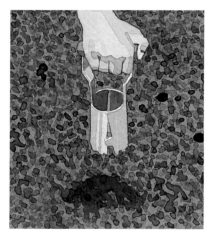

2 Place the bulb in the hole, then squeeze the handle of the bulb planter to release the soil back into the planting hole. Firm down.

1 Alternatively, dig a hole two or three times the depth of the bulbs. On heavy soils, add a layer of gravel to aid drainage.

2 Set the bulbs in, spacing them twice their own width apart to allow for the production of offsets.

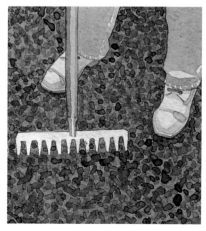

3 Fill in carefully around the bulbs to avoid disturbing them. Firm down with the back of a rake and label.

PLANTING BULBS IN POTS AND TUBS

  !! 10 MINS PER POT

- Pots and tubs are quick and easy to plant up
- Planting in layers provides extra impact and can prolong the season of interest

Pots filled with spring bulbs bring life and colour to the patio. The basic planting method is very quick and easy, and the bulbs can be left in their pots for two or three seasons or transferred to the garden (*see p.61*).
■ Delay planting tulips until mid- to late autumn.

▲ *This rich blue and yellow scheme uses hyacinths planted up with hardy primulas.*

1 Crock the base of terracotta pots to ensure good drainage. This is vital for spring bulbs, which can rot in cold, over-moist conditions, especially in winter.

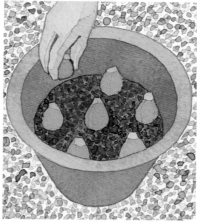

2 Fill the base of the pot with free-draining, loam-based compost. Set the bulbs in at twice their own depth, spacing them a bulb's width apart.

3 Top up with compost to within 2.5cm (1in) of the rim and cover with a layer of gravel. Label, water and set outdoors in a sheltered position.

TIPS

❀ Terracotta provides bulbs with excellent insulation against winter cold, but when buying opt for the better-quality pots that are guaranteed frost proof, to prevent breakages.

❀ Check the compost of planted pots during dry spells in winter, watering moderately if necessary.

❀ Feed with a high-potash fertilizer at the recommended rate when leaves emerge to boost flowering, and again when the flowers have died off, to help feed the bulbs.

Planting a mix of varieties (with each bulb at twice its own depth) provides a succession of flowers.

For mass displays of one variety, set a layer of bulbs at three times their own depth and a second layer above it.

OVERWINTERING TENDER PERENNIALS

  5 MINS PER PLANT

• **Overwintering cuts the costs of bedding displays by growing on the more expensive varieties**
• **Once potted up, aftercare in winter is minimal**
• **Zonal geraniums provide extra colour indoors through winter**

Tender perennials such as geraniums (*Pelargonium*), fuchsias and marguerites (*Argyranthemum*) are invaluable for summer displays, but they can be expensive. To cut costs, simply bring them in before frosts threaten and overwinter them indoors, ready for potting up and growing on next spring (*see p.24*). Zonal geraniums (those with a faint maroon 'horseshoe' mark on the leaf) can be kept in a warm room and will often continue to flower, providing a little extra indoor colour through winter. Other types of geranium, and other tender perennials, are best overwintered in cool, frost-free conditions. Some, like fuchsias, shed their leaves and undergo a period of dormancy. All plants kept in cool conditions should be watered very infrequently, and dormant plants can be left to dry out completely before watering moderately.

1 If the plant (here, zonal geranium) is in a mixed planting, remove the container, then carefully ease away any annuals and discard them. Try to retain as much root as possible.

2 Select a pot that is only a little larger than the root ball. Set the plant in, checking that it is a snug fit, then push compost down the side of the pot to fill any gaps. Firm it down and water well.

3 Prune back the main stems by approximately half, and cut out any stems that are congesting the centre of the plant. Cutting above an outward-facing bud will ensure new growth.

4 For flowers through winter, place the pot in a warm, light position indoors and keep moderately watered. Otherwise, set plants in a light, frost-free spot and water only if the compost is bone dry.

TIPS

❀ For ease when separating plants, and to minimize root damage, water the container an hour or so before dismantling it. Similarly, water any border-grown plants before lifting them. Moist roots are much easier to handle.

❀ If potted-up plants are taking up an inordinate amount of space indoors, it is also possible to overwinter tender perennials from semi-ripe cuttings taken in mid- to late summer (*see p.69*). These will require pots up to 9cm (3½in).

❀ There is no need to cut back fuchsias and marguerites – pruning can be carried out in spring (*see p.24*).

❀ Other tender perennials that can be overwintered successfully include nemesias, osteospermums, verbena, plectranthus and scaevola.

❀ Plants that are already in individual pots should simply be bought indoors and cut back. There is no need to repot them either now or in spring (*see p.24*).

▲ *Marguerites are easy to overwinter.*

CREATING A LAWN FROM SEED

 !!! 5 MINS PER SQ M/YD

• Sowing seed is light, easy work compared to turfing
• Seed is extremely cost-effective, particularly for large areas
• There is a wide range of grass mixes for all situations
• Sowing seed in autumn helps cut down on aftercare

Creating a lawn from seed has several advantages over laying turf (*see p.38*); it is lighter work, much cheaper, and there is a good selection of seed mixes suitable for all grades of wear, and for sunny and shady sites. The only drawback is that it will be three or four months before the lawn can be used. To ensure that the grass establishes well, keep it watered until it is growing strongly. When it reaches approximately 5cm (2in) high, remove the net and mow with the blades set high, gradually decreasing the height of cut with each mowing until a dense sward is achieved.

■ Seed can also be sown in spring, but there will be more competition from weeds, and drier weather will necessitate more frequent watering.

 TIPS

✿ To ensure an even mix of grasses, stir the seed before sowing it.

✿ For speedier sowing, use a lawn spreader. Weigh out the total seed needed for the area, and sow half in one direction, half in the other.

✿ Do not walk on the lawn until it is well established, except for any necessary mowing or weeding.

✿ Deal with perennial weeds quickly, so that they do not deter grass growth. Carefully pull or dig them out, or apply a lawn spot-weeder (*see p.131*).

▲ *Careful seeding and aftercare creates a lush, dense lawn.*

1 Prepare the ground (*see pp.36–37*), then mark out the area into 1 sq m/yd sections using pegs and line.

2 Stir the seed and weigh the recommended amount per sq m/yd. Place in a plastic cup and mark the level.

3 To ensure an even cover within each grid square, scatter half of the seed in one direction and the remainder at right angles to it.

4 To improve germination, lightly rake the seed into the top surface of the soil. Water well and keep watered through any dry spells.

5 To protect the site from birds, who will use it for dust-bathing as well as taking the seed, cover with fine mesh netting and peg it in place.

POTTING UP HERBS FOR WINTER USE

5 MINS PER POT

- Lifting, dividing and potting up is quick and simple
- Ensures plentiful supplies of herbs through winter, by providing a little extra heat for those that would normally die back
- It is suitable for a number of popular herbs
- Aftercare is minimal, involving only occasional watering

Many herbs will grow quite happily indoors for instant winter harvesting. Most valuable of all are those that die back in the garden through winter such as mint and chives. Given warmer conditions indoors, they will carry on growing so that the fresh-picked flavour can be enjoyed all-year round. Tarragon, marjoram and lemon balm also die back in winter and can be lifted and potted for growing on indoors. Grow plants on in a cool, well-lit position – an unheated porch or conservatory is ideal. Keep all herbs moderately watered, making sure that the compost is moist but not saturated.

TIPS

❀ For easy lifting and division, wait until the soil is moist, or water plants thoroughly an hour or so beforehand.

❀ To ensure regular supplies of the most popular herbs, plant up two or three pots. Harvest from one pot at a time, leaving the remainder to grow on.

❀ Herbs that have been forced through winter can be replanted in the garden in spring, but the forcing process is very taxing and they should be left unharvested for a year, to give them time to recover.

▶ *Ginger mint is both useful and decorative, with its attractive variegation.*

For a supply of chives through winter, lift a clump and divide off one or two sections, discarding any damaged bulbs. Replace the main clump and water well to settle it back in.

1 Loosen the soil around a clump of mint, ease out a stem with a good root system, then firm back the soil. Trim back the roots of the selected portions so that they will fit the pot.

2 Place crocks in the base of terracotta pots, then pot up the herbs using a loam-based compost. Fill up with more compost to within 1cm (½in) of the rim, firm down and water well.

3 Trim back the plants to encourage fresh growth and grow on outdoors. Bring the pots indoors when frosts are forecast and place in a well-lit position for winter harvesting.

PLANTING SPRING CABBAGES

 | **!** | 15 MINS PER 12 PLANTS | ◗

- **Spring cabbages are easy, undemanding crops, at their most nutritious when freshly picked**
- **Growing cabbages makes good use of empty ground in winter, as a follow-on from summer crops**
- **Close planting and staggered harvesting provide both spring greens and hearted cabbages**

Spring cabbages are tasty and nutritious, and very easy to grow. They also make good use of vacant ground in the kitchen garden, which would otherwise lie fallow through winter. If the soil was well prepared for the previous crop, no further preparation is necessary; digging over is counter-productive, because cabbages grow best on a firm soil, and over-fertilizing causes lush growth which can suffer in winter. Cabbages prefer an open, sunny position, and this is especially important for spring cabbages, which have to contend with the lower light levels and shorter days of winter.

TIPS

✽ For a mix of spring greens and hearted spring lettuce, space plants only 10–15cm (4–6in) apart. Harvest intermediate plants as loose-leaved spring greens, letting the remainder heart up for harvesting through to early summer.

✽ Cabbages need a good deal of moisture, so water them well through any prolonged dry spells in spring.

✽ For even earlier crops, cover the cabbage patch with horticultural fleece in late winter to provide a little extra warmth. Remove when the weather warms up in spring.

▶ *Spring cabbages are a useful, easy and nutritious crop.*

1 Using a trowel to make planting holes, set purchased or home-grown cabbage seedlings 30cm (1ft) apart in staggered rows, so that the plants are equidistant. Firm down well and water thoroughly.

2 To foil cabbage root fly, which can devastate crops, slip a cabbage collar around each plant. This prevents the larvae, which are laid on the surface, from tunnelling down into the roots, causing plants to collapse.

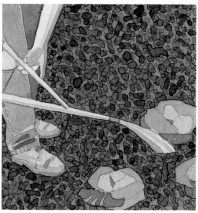

3 Feed plants with a high-nitrogen fertilizer in early spring to boost growth. Liquid feeds are the quickest-acting, and can be watered in around the plant or sprayed onto the leaves.

4 Begin to harvest in early spring. To obtain a second, smaller crop from each plant, cut a shallow cross in the stump. As many as three or four small heads will develop from the cut portion.

MID-AUTUMN

As the weather cools, so the gardening pace begins to hot up after the relative calm of summer and early autumn. Autumn plantings can begin, evergreens can be transplanted, and climbing roses will be even lovelier next year if carefully pruned now. There is all the plant debris from autumn pruning and cutting back to be considered too, and there are several ways to make best use of this valuable material. Finally, try to spare a little time for planting containers for winter and spring colour – it is quick work, and very rewarding.

▲ Autumn berries of Sorbus cashmiriana.

PRUNING FOR WIND PROTECTION

  !!! 5–15 MINS PER PLANT

• **Pruning now minimizes any damage that could be caused by winter gales**
• **The pruning method is very quick and simple**

Plants such as bush roses, and late flowering shrubs, like buddleja and lavatera, can become top-heavy by the end of summer. In more exposed gardens, these plants are very vulnerable to winter gales. If left unpruned, they will be buffeted by strong winds and the resultant rocking action can cause enormous damage by tearing the root system. By simply reducing the height of the plant, you will be minimizing the leverage effect.

1 Using secateurs, remove any spindly stems. At the same time, cut out any dead or diseased growth to prevent problems from spreading during winter.

2 Cut back the remaining top-growth by approximately one-quarter (or slightly more for very long stems), making a slanting cut just above a leaf joint.

TIPS

❀ To save the time involved in cutting back, try to site taller plants in more sheltered positions in future, well away from the prevailing wind.

❀ The full pruning of buddleja, lavatera and bush roses is undertaken in spring (*see pp.18–19*).

▶ *Cut back tall, free-flowering lavatera to reduce the risk of wind-rock.*

TRANSPLANTING EVERGREEN SHRUBS AND CONIFERS

  !! 45 MINS FOR LARGE PLANTS

- **Transplantation 'recycles' valuable evergreen shrubs and conifers that are failing to thrive**
- **It can also considerably improve the garden layout**

As gardens develop, there often comes a stage when you discover that a plant has been set in the wrong position. It might be a sun-lover struggling in a shady spot, a plant that has outgrown its allotted space, one that is being crowded out by other plants, or one that simply looks out of place. Fortunately, moving plants is not as risky as you might think. Younger plants can be transplanted easily, and although older, larger plants take longer to re-establish and need more ongoing care, even these can be moved successfully. It is vital to protect them from harsh, drying winds through their first winter, by draping them with horticultural fleece, and to keep them watered through any dry spells during their first spring and summer.

■ Deciduous shrubs can be moved at any time after leaf fall, from late autumn to early spring.

TIPS

❀ In dry weather, water the ground thoroughly a day before transplanting. This makes digging much easier, especially on heavy soils, and helps to reduce the amount of root damage.

❀ Get someone to help if you are planning to transplant extra-large specimens – it will save a good deal of time and effort.

❀ Small shrubs and conifers are even easier to move. Simply dig around the plant at an angle of 45°, retaining as much root ball as possible, and carry it on a spade to the new planting spot.

1 Mark a circle around the plant (here, rhododendron) under the outermost spread of the branches, and dig a narrow trench around the circle.

2 Gently fork away some soil from the root ball to reduce its size and its weight. Smaller plants, with less cumbersome root balls, can be left intact.

3 Cut under the root ball with a spade, severing any thick roots if necessary. Now lever up the root ball and slide a sheet of polythene underneath it.

4 Lever up the other side of the root ball, pull the polythene through and tie the corners of the sheet onto the stem to secure the root ball.

5 Dig a new planting hole at the same depth as the root ball but twice the diameter. Loosen the base with a fork and add a thin layer of organic matter.

6 Position the plant flush with the soil, remove the polythene and fill in with a soil/organic matter mix. Firm in, water well and mulch with bark chips.

PLANTING A CLEMATIS THROUGH A TREE

| | ! | 20 MINS PER PLANT | ◑ |

• **Clematis can look wonderful planted through trees**
• **Once they reach the tree canopy, no further support is needed**

Clematis is one of the best loved of all flowering climbers, and can look lovely planted through a tree, so long as you match tree and clematis carefully. Neat, spring-flowering *Clematis alpina* and *C. macropetala* are perfect for small trees. The popular large-flowered hybrids, flowering at any time between late spring and early autumn, are rather more vigorous and will need a taller host – an old apple or pear tree is ideal. Plenty of moisture is the major requirement for young clematis plants, and they should be watered regularly through any dry spells in winter and during their first spring and summer.

TIPS

❀ Soak the plant thoroughly before planting, and tease out any circling roots before setting it in.

❀ The particularly deep planting is an insurance against clematis wilt (a sudden and total collapse), since the plant will usually regenerate from underground stems.

❀ It is best to position the clematis on the shady side of the tree to provide a cool root run. If this is not possible, shade the roots with paving slabs, or with low-growing shrubs or hardy perennials.

❀ If the soil from the planting hole is very poor, replace it entirely, using good garden soil mixed with organic matter to help retain moisture.

▶ *With its neat habit, summer-flowering C. 'Comtesse de Bouchaud' is ideal for growing through smaller trees.*

1 Water the clematis well. Dig a 45 x 45cm (18 x 18in) hole at least 45cm (18in) from the tree. Fork the base and add a layer of organic matter.

2 Mix the excavated soil with organic matter and set the clematis in so that the top of the root ball is 10cm (4in) below the level of the surrounding soil.

3 Fill in with the soil mix, firm down well, and tie clematis netting around the trunk of the tree to guide the plant into the lower branches. Tie the stems to a sturdy cane, angled in to the netting.

4 Mulch around the plant with bark chips to help retain moisture. For effective watering, sink a 25cm (10in) pot next to it, to ensure that water goes directly to the root ball. Water well.

PRUNING CLIMBING ROSES

 !!! 20–30 MINS PER PLANT

- **Annual pruning promotes healthier, more shapely plants**
- **The occasional removal of main stems encourages strong renewal growth from the base**

Climbing roses are a wonderful way to cover walls and pergolas, and those that flower continuously, or produce a second flush of flower in autumn, are especially good value in smaller gardens. Unless they make very vigorous growth, climbing roses should not be pruned until their third year. This is particularly important with climbing forms of bush roses, such as 'Climbing Iceberg' which, if cut hard back in the early stages, can revert to the bush form. Thereafter, pruning is simply a matter of common sense, to remove unsightly growth, to tidy up the whole plant so that it will look its best next year, and to encourage replacement stems on plants that have become leggy.

TIPS

✿ It is important to tie in all new stems after pruning, while they are still fairly whippy. If you leave the job until next year, they can be very stiff and awkward to handle, especially if you want to train them horizontally.

✿ For quick and easy collection of prunings, lay a polythene sheet at the foot of the plant.

✿ Some climbing roses are more prone to legginess than others. The alternative to cutting out one or two older stems every few years is to plant a shrub or perennial in front of the rose to mask the unsightly bare stems.

➤ *A robust, climbing rose, with heavily scented blooms in early summer,* Rosa *'Alchymist' should be pruned in mid-autumn.*

1 When the rose has finished flowering, cut out any twiggy, dead or damaged growth, taking it back to the main stem. Prune back any stems that have started to die back, cutting 5–8cm (2–3in) into healthy green wood.

2 Cut back all sideshoots to within approximately 10–15cm (4–6in) of the main stem, making the cut above an outward-facing bud. This will encourage shapely growth next year and an even cover of foliage and flowers.

3 Prune back any over-long main stems to keep them within the allotted space. Tie in any long new stems, training them horizontally where possible, to encourage maximum flowering.

✿ If the plant is bare and leggy at its base, cut out one or two of the older stems to within 30cm (1ft) of the ground to encourage vigorous new stems from the base.

ROCK GARDEN CLEAR-UP

  !!! 10 MINS PER SESSION ▶

- **A quick clear-up shows plants to their best advantage**
- **Removing fallen leaves protects vulnerable plants from rot**

The rock garden often looks a little jaded by mid-autumn as flowering diminishes and herbaceous plants begin to die back. Alpines are normally displayed as single specimens against a background of top-dressing, so that any dishevelled plants are particularly noticeable. Happily, a quick clear-up soon gets the whole rock garden back into shape, and keeps it looking neat and well kempt through winter. Rot is the major enemy of alpines, and particularly of succulent varieties such as sedums and sempervivums. For these plants, the regular removal of fallen leaves is vital. The other simple precaution you can take against rot for all alpine plants is to renew the top-dressing if it has become thin or patchy (*see p.16*). Fresh top-dressing ensures sharp drainage through the wettest winter.

TIPS

❀ It is a wise precaution to leave a slight stem cover of 5–8cm (2–3in) when cutting back herbaceous alpines in autumn. This little extra cover will protect the crowns of alpines that are on the borderline of hardiness and help reduce losses from frost damage.

❀ Evergreen helianthemum (the floriferous rock rose) benefits from being cut back by half in autumn. This encourages a densely bushy growth habit and more, and better, flowers next year.

▶ *A few simple tasks keep the rock garden looking neat and well-groomed through autumn and winter.*

Clear away fallen leaves regularly, especially if they are lying on plants, since leaves create a moist environment where rot can develop. The removal of leaves also keeps the rock garden neat.

Using a sharp knife, carefully cut away any dead rosettes from saxifrages and similar plants, making the cut right at the base of the rosette. Put a little top-dressing into the ensuing gap.

Using shears for speed and ease, clip plants to remove all faded flower stems (here, thyme). At the same time, clip back any straggly foliage, to keep plants neat and shapely.

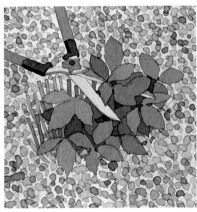

Shear back the dead top-growth of herbaceous alpines (here, astilbe) to within 5–8cm (2–3in) of the ground. Dead foliage is a favourite hiding place for slugs in winter.

POND MAINTENANCE

  !!! 20 MINS PER SMALL POND

• **Cutting back is quick and easy work that instantly improves the look of the pond**
• **The removal of dying foliage and fallen leaves prevents them from polluting the water**

Pond plants are beginning to look tired now, and cutting back those that die down in winter serves two purposes: it improves the whole look of the pond by removing unsightly, collapsing vegetation, and it prevents the dead and dying leaves from polluting the water. Fallen leaves from surrounding trees will also sully the water if not regularly removed. Both jobs are very simple and relatively quick, and they will also help to prevent the build-up of sludge in the bottom of the pond. If this sludge becomes very thick, it will eventually necessitate a wholesale (and tiresome) emptying and dredging operation.

TIPS

❀ At the same time as cutting back marginal plants, remove the spent leaves and flowers of waterlilies, and thin out oxygenators if they have become congested (*see p.67*).

❀ If there are fish in the pond, they are more vulnerable to predators when much of the vegetation has been cleared. Provide a little protection by laying short sections of drainpipe in which they can hide.

▲ *Cutting back faded marginal plants keeps the pond both healthy and tidy.*

Using secateurs, cut back the faded top-growth of herbaceous marginal plants to prevent the dying leaves from polluting the water.

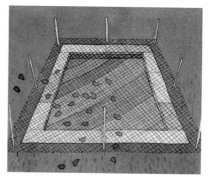

Keep the pond free of fallen leaves from nearby trees. Netting smaller ponds is much easier than scooping the leaves out on a daily basis.

SAVING SEED

   ! 5–10 MINS PER PLANT

• **Saving and storing seed is very easy and cuts costs**

Saving seed is a simple operation, and a good way of ensuring fresh stocks of favourite plants, particularly annuals and biennials.

TIPS

❀ Seedheads that are still soft and fleshy can be left to ripen on sheets of blotting paper or paper towel.

❀ Always store seed in paper bags or envelopes (never plastic) and keep in cool, dry conditions.

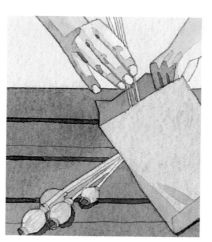

Some plants (here, poppy) shed seed very readily. They can be collected by simply putting the seedheads into a paper bag and shaking them, then transferring the seed to a labelled envelope to store until needed.

For plants that do not shed seed quite so readily (here, hollyhock), pick whole seedheads when they are fully ripe and carefully dismantle them over a plate, removing the seed and separating it from any debris.

RECYCLING PLANT WASTE

  30 MINS MAX PER TASK

• **Grass clippings and leafy waste provide valuable material for the compost heap**

• **A shredder quickly chops up both leafy and woody waste, for adding to the compost heap, or for use as an excellent mulch**

Even the smallest garden can generate a surprising amount of waste, and almost all of it can be recycled to provide valuable material when digging new ground, for composting, and for use as a mulch. Grass clippings and leafy waste can be added to the compost heap (*see facing page*), together with chopped pieces of whippy prunings. Woodier waste, with stems up to about 2.5cm (1in) thick, can be processed with a garden shredder, saving a good deal of money on mulching material. The shredder can also be used for leafier material, chopping it up so that it breaks down very quickly when added to the compost heap.

TIPS

❀ If a lot of whippy prunings have accumulated for chopping into smaller pieces, take the leisurely approach. Pull up a chair and chop them into a large bag or bucket, ready for transfer to the compost heap.

❀ Wear gloves and goggles when operating a shredder, as protection against thorny stems and flying debris. Use the shredder at sociable hours, since they can be very noisy (although 'silent' models are slowly becoming available, which also use less power).

❀ Shredders can be quite heavy, so for ease and manoeuvrability, opt for a wheeled model.

▷ *Composting makes best use of suitable kitchen and garden waste.*

Young, pliable stems of trees and shrubs can be added to the compost heap, along with kitchen and garden waste. If chopped up finely, they will soon rot down.

When digging over new ground (*see p.107*), line the trenches with a 5–8cm (2–3in) layer of leafy garden waste. It will break down to help improve the condition of the soil.

A shredder makes short work of woody waste such as hedge and shrub prunings. The resulting material can be used as a valuable mulch, or added to the compost heap to break down further.

If a shredder is not available, bag up woody waste and dispose of it rather than burning it. Bonfires pollute the atmosphere, and the smoke can be a nuisance to neighbours.

MAKING COMPOST

  !! 30 MINS MAX PER TASK

• **Compost-making recycles a wide range of kitchen and garden waste**
• **The resulting compost mulch is invaluable as a soil conditioner**

Although it is not the most glamorous of materials, there is something very satisfying about making compost, turning all kinds of kitchen and garden waste into a rich, crumbly material that will benefit the garden enormously. Fill the bin so that there is a good mix of sappy and more solid materials, and keep wooden bins covered with polythene or old carpet. If using a lot of drier material, water the heap so that it is evenly moist but not saturated, to speed decomposition. Proprietary compost activators will also aid the decomposition process, as will thin layers of garden soil or fresh manure. Well-made compost is invaluable for digging in to improve soil condition and can also be used as an excellent mulch.

TIPS

❀ Most organic matter can be added to the heap, including shredded newspaper to bulk it out.

❀ The only materials to avoid are meat, which attracts rodents, weeds that have set seed, the roots of perennial weeds such as bindweed, and diseased plant material, which can survive the composting process and re-infect the garden.

❀ If you want to save the time involved in turning the compost heap, simply empty it out when most of the material has rotted down, forking any drier, less decomposed material into the base of a new heap.

▶ *Several bins will produce a constant supply of home-made compost.*

1 Add kitchen and garden waste to the compost bin in layers, spreading it evenly to avoid air pockets. Scatter grass clippings across the heap, rather than leaving them as a solid mass, which will become slimy and unpleasant.

2 To accelerate the composting process, sprinkle the heap with a liquid or granular compost activator every 15–23cm (6–9in) or so, or add a thin layer of organic matter. Keep the bin covered when not in use.

3 For best results, turn the heap after a few weeks. Empty it out, then pile the base with the browner, crumbly material, forking drier material into the centre of the heap.

Plastic, open-based compost bins also work well: pyramidal models are the easiest to lift off when the heap needs turning. A hatch is convenient for the removal of compost.

PLANTING FOR WINTER AND SPRING COLOUR

  ! 20 MINS PER LARGE POT

• **Winter plantings need only a minimum of care**
• **Spring flowers and bulbs can be added to plantings to extend the season of interest**

After the vivid displays of summer bedding plants, the patio can look a little dull and flat in autumn. To give it extra life and sparkle, plant up a few pots to provide colour through winter and on into spring. Planting up is quick and easy, and winter container plantings need very little care – simply dead-head flowering plants now and again, and water moderately if the compost begins to dry out. Feeding is not necessary, as plants grow very slowly in winter. The range of plants for winter flower, foliage and berry colour is enormous, with winter pansies being one of the most valuable sources of bright colour. Adding in spring plants such as bulbs, primulas and bellis daisies (*Bellis perennis*) will extend the life of the planting.

TIPS

❀ The easiest pots to plant up are those that have a good number of evergreens (conifers, young shrubs and ivy, for instance) underplanted with winter bedding plants. In late spring, it is an easy matter to scrap the bedding plants and replace them with summer varieties.

❀ To maximize the pleasure from planted pots, place them where they can be seen from house windows.

❀ Include a few hyacinth bulbs when planting up window boxes, to relish their delicious fragrance on warm spring days.

▶ *Skimmias are invaluable for their attractive winter flowers and berries.*

1 Extra-sharp drainage is absolutely vital for winter plantings, so place a generous layer of crocks or gravel in the base of terracotta pots. This prevents the single drainage hole from becoming blocked by compost.

2 Line the pot with free-draining, loam-based compost, then plant a layer of bulbs, which will provide extra colour and pleasure in spring. Set them in a circle at twice their own depth and 5cm (2in) apart.

3 Cover the bulbs with compost to within 5–8cm (2–3in) of the rim, then place an evergreen (here, skimmia) in the centre, settling it in so that the top of the root ball is flush with the compost.

4 Set plants like winter pansies around the edge of the pot, interspersing them with winter- and spring-flowering plants such as hardy primulas. Top up the compost if necessary, and water well.

REPAIRING LAWN EDGES

   !!! 15 MINS PER PATCH

- **Repairing edges in autumn keeps lawns looking good through the winter months, when any defects are so much more obvious**
- **The 'cut and turn' method is quick, easy and effective**

Lawn edges can be damaged in a number of ways, and it is often in autumn, as the surrounding plants die back, that they are most noticeable. One of the commonest causes is boisterous children or pets, but border plants can also create problems. If they are allowed to flop over onto the lawn, they shade out the grass, leaving a bald patch that can be very dry and crumbly. Rebuilding and reseeding the edge of a lawn that directly adjoins border soil is tricky work. The 'cut and turn' method is considerably easier and more successful.

■ Lawn edges can also be repaired in spring. Summer repairs will entail extra care in keeping the seed and young grass watered.

TIPS

❀ Repair lawn edges when the soil is moist – the turf is easier to cut and undercut, and there is less likelihood of it breaking when turned.

❀ If the soil is poor, add a little granular fertilizer before reseeding.

❀ Use a seed type appropriate for the lawn and situation. Small packs of mixes are now available, including those for shade, and for all types of grass from luxury to heavy duty.

❀ In future summers, use link stakes to prevent plants from flopping directly onto the lawn (see p.30).

▶ *Neat, crisp edges are essential if the lawn is to look its best through autumn and winter.*

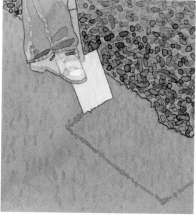
1 Using a sharp spade, cut out a rectangle of turf around the damaged area. Cut by eye, or take a rectangular piece of card, lay it on the turf held down with a brick, and use it as a template.

2 Carefully undercut the turf with the spade to a depth of at least 2.5cm (1in), then turn the turf round so that it faces inwards, taking care not to break it. Firm down well.

3 Fill up the gaps in the damaged area with good garden soil or loam-based compost, levelling it off and firming it down. Sow a seed and compost mix and water well.

4 Cover the area with fine mesh netting so that the seed is not taken by birds. Keep it watered through any dry spells, and remove the netting when the seed has germinated.

LATE AUTUMN

There is a marked change in the weather in late autumn, with the first real frosts and the possibility of strong winds. The garden seems to cower a little, evergreen plants drooping miserably when nipped by frost. It is an in-between time, and the gardener's job is to ease the transition into winter as smoothly as possible. Planting is still possible, and new ground can be dug over, but most important of all is the work you can do now to prevent winter damage – a chore when it is cold and wet, but a pleasure on a fine brisk day.

▲ *Pampas grass and conifers on a frosty day.*

WIND PROTECTION

   !!! 20 MINS MAX PER TASK

• **A few sensible precautions will reduce the damage caused by autumn and winter winds, and the time and cost involved in repairs**

The high winds of autumn and winter can wreak havoc in the garden, but a few simple measures will help to minimize any damage. Newly planted trees are especially vulnerable, and should always be securely staked (*see facing page*). If they are not firmly anchored, wind-rock can cause damage to the root system. Climbers, too, are easily damaged if the ties are not secure, or if any long, loose stems have not been tied in. At the same time, you can check for any over-tight ties that are threatening to bite into the stems. Examine garden structures too. A rotted fence post, for example, is easily fixed (*see p.76*), whereas a fallen fence can cause a lot of damage that will take time and trouble to put right. Repairs can be costly too, so check whether plants and structures are covered by your insurance policy.

▶ *Protect roses such as 'Climbing Iceberg', which can flower right through to mid-winter, by tying in any loose stems.*

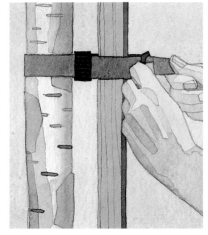

1 Check that all tree ties are secure so that they are not rocked by wind and the roots damaged. This is also a good opportunity to check for any ties that have become over-tight and need slackening off.

2 Climbers can suffer considerable damage in windy weather if they are not well fastened to their supports. Check that all existing ties are secure, and tie in any long, loose stems, using plastic-coated wire ties.

TIPS

❀ Close the doors and windows of sheds and greenhouses in windy weather. If left open, they create a 'funnelling' effect; causing extensive damage that may not be covered by your insurance policy.

❀ The combination of ground frost and constant high wind can dry out newly planted evergreens, which are losing water from the leaves and cannot take it up from the ground. Draping them with horticultural fleece will reduce the rate of transpiration.

PLANTING A BARE-ROOT TREE

   !!! 20 MINS PER TREE

- **Bare-root trees are the most cost-effective**
- **If well planted, trees are the most labour-saving of all plants, needing a minimum of care**

Trees are one of the most important garden features. They have great presence, and can be used to provide shade, shelter and privacy, as well as making lovely 'stand-alone' specimens. Most trees have an indefinite life span, they are generally very healthy, and they are extremely labour-saving, rarely needing any special care or attention. Bare-root trees are available in autumn and can be very cost-effective compared to container-grown plants, especially if you are planting several. The stark, bare roots may not look promising, but they establish remarkably quickly and easily, providing that care is taken when planting and that they are kept watered in any dry spells in their first spring and summer. Very young bare-root trees (single-stemmed 'whips') are the best value of all. Although small, they will grow more quickly than older trees. Only deciduous trees are supplied bare-root.

1 Soak the tree roots in a large bucket while preparing the planting hole. Dig a hole that will comfortably accommodate the roots, and mix the excavated soil with organic matter.

2 Drive in a stake so that it is 60cm (2ft) above the ground, then mound soil mix in the hole. Set the tree in, spread the roots, and check that the dark 'soil mark' is at ground level.

3 Fill in with the soil mix, settling it carefully around the roots and firming it down well at all stages. This gives the roots a good foothold, and ensures there are no air pockets.

4 Attach the tree to the top of the stake, using an adjustable tree tie with a buffer to prevent chafing. Place a thick mulch, such as bark chips, around the tree and water well.

TIPS

❀ When planting a tree as a lawn specimen, always leave a wide circle (at least 1m/3ft) of bare earth around the base, to allow for feeding and mulching, and to give the roots their fair share of nutrients and water – grass is surprisingly competitive.

❀ Low stakes allow the top of the tree to move in the wind. This slight motion encourages a better, more wide-spreading root system and helps to promote a stable, tapered trunk. Leave the stake in place for the first two years.

❀ Bare-root trees are safe in their wrapping for up to a week. If planting is delayed, plant them up temporarily in spare ground in a sheltered position, keeping them well watered.

❀ If necessary, use a tree guard to protect young trees from rabbits and other wild animals, which can strip both bark and leaves.

❀ If you prefer to buy a container-grown tree, use the same planting method as for a shrub (see p.83).

▲ A vigorous, well-planted young apple tree.

PLANTING A BARE-ROOT ROSE

  !!! 15–20 MINS PER PLANT

• **Bare-root roses can be very good value when bought from garden centres and DIY stores**
• **Mail order specialists stock bare-root supplies of a wide range of roses, including the rarer varieties**

Garden centres stock an excellent range of bare-root roses in autumn and they are very good value. Mail order rose specialists send out bare-root stocks at this time too, and have a much wider range – mail order is often the only way to obtain supplies of less common varieties. When planting, it is vital that the graft union is below ground level or the plant will send up a forest of suckers from the rootstock (*see p.68*).

TIPS

❀ Place orders for roses by mail well in advance. Demand can outstrip supply, especially of the more unusual varieties, or of any that have been only recently been introduced.

❀ If possible, carefully inspect bare-root roses before purchase. They should have at least three or four sturdy, healthy looking shoots, with no sign of disease or die-back, and an evenly spaced root system.

❀ Save a good deal of aggravation by not planting roses on ground where roses were previously grown. They will suffer from replant sickness – not fully understood by the scientists, but all too real – and will make poor, stunted specimens. If you are determined to plant roses on old rosebeds, you will need to dig out a 60 x 60cm (2 x 2ft) cube of soil and replace it with loam-based compost, topsoil or fresh soil from elsewhere in the garden.

▶ *One of the oldest gallica roses, pink-striped R. gallica 'Versicolor' (syn. 'Rosa Mundi') has great charm.*

1 Soak the roots in a large bucket for an hour or so and meanwhile dig a planting hole that will accommodate the roots with ease. Mix the excavated soil with good organic matter.

2 Remove the rose from the water and trim off any twiggy or damaged stems, then reduce the longest roots by approximately one-third to encourage a vigorous, well-branched root system.

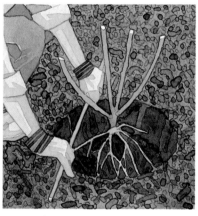

3 Set the rose in the planting hole and spread out the roots. Use a cane to check that the knobbly graft union between roots and top-growth is 2.5cm (1in) below ground level.

4 Fill in with the soil mix, firming it in around the roots and firming again at every stage of filling the hole, to avoid leaving air pockets. Finally, mulch around the plant and water well.

AUTUMN CLEAR-UP

  !!! 1 HOUR PER SMALL GARDEN ●

• A thorough clear-up in late autumn removes clutter and keeps the garden looking good in winter
• Leaving well-structured perennials unpruned until spring can add interest to the winter garden

The garden can begin to look tired and a little unkempt by late autumn, but a quick clearance session will soon get it back into shape, so that it looks tidy and well cared for over the winter. Clearing away faded top-growth of herbaceous perennials makes an instant improvement, and clearing rose leaves, together with removing any leaves from low, cushion-forming evergreens helps to keep plants healthy. Finally, a good sweep-up of paths and patios makes a huge difference. The garden may not be at its most glamorous in winter, but it can be quietly pleasing.

TIPS

❀ Always use secateurs to remove faded stems, rather than pulling them off. Whole sections of clump-forming perennials can be lifted out of the ground if pulled.

❀ Leave the top-growth of those herbaceous perennials that remain decorative through winter. Grasses, ice plant (*Sedum spectabile*), and sea holly (*Eryngium*) are just some of the many perennials that retain their structure and form, giving a little extra interest to the winter garden.

❀ Remove, or spot-treat, any weeds on paved areas (*see p.25*). If the soil has become compacted since the interim border clear-up in early autumn, fork it over lightly to open it up (*see p.82*).

▶ *The garden can look lovely in autumn, providing that you spare a little time to keep it reasonably tidy.*

Clear away faded or dead top-growth of hardy perennials. The clippings make excellent material for the compost heap. Plants that have died back completely should be cut back to within 5–8cm (2–3in) of the ground.

Clear away any fallen leaves lying on low-growing evergreens such as thyme or pinks (*Dianthus*). If left on the plant through the cold and wet of winter, they trap moisture, which can cause fungal attack and subsequent rot.

Leaves on border soil can be left to rot down naturally. The exception is rose leaves; if plants have suffered from rust or blackspot, they can be reinfected by the fallen leaves, so gather them up with a rake and dispose of them.

Sweep up any plant debris and soil on paved areas, lifting or moving pots in order to sweep under them. This removes the litter that is a favourite hiding place for pests, and gives a neater appearance to the whole garden.

CARING FOR WILDLIFE

  15–20 MINS MAX PER TASK

• **Birds that are regularly fed will use the garden as a base and clean up many insect pests**
• **Attractive berrying shrubs and trees will supplement their diet in autumn and winter**
• **Frogs will help keep down the local slug population**

Looking after local wildlife has many rewards, and birds, in particular, are both entertaining and useful garden visitors. They are enjoyable to watch, as they squabble and queue for food, but when the bird table is empty, they will stay in the vicinity and peck up great quantities of insect pests such as aphids and caterpillars. Putting out a mix of foods, including nuts, seeds and kitchen scraps, will attract the widest range. Frogs are useful too, with their fondness for slugs, and even the smallest pond will attract them in great numbers.

TIPS

❀ Peanuts should not be provided during spring and summer when birds are nesting. They are not suitable for fledglings, which can choke on them.

❀ To keep birds safe from cats, set the bird table in an open area, away from overhanging trees.

❀ Site bird boxes in a shady position out of the prevailing wind and well away from any smothering bonfire smoke. A house wall, where they are safe from agile predators, such as squirrels, is ideal.

❀ Many creatures, from frogs to field mice, can take up residence in the compost heap, so be extra-careful when emptying it.

▶ *Blue tits and great tits are especially fond of peanuts, while starlings will eat anything that is put out for them.*

Encourage a diverse range of birds to the garden by installing a bird table and putting out a varied selection of foods. A table with a roof will keep food rather drier in wet weather.

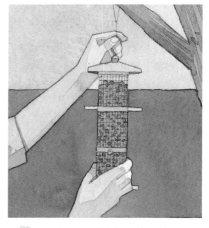
Supplement bird table food by hanging up feeders filled with nuts and seeds. Hanging feeders are useful if there are cats about, since the birds are safely out of their way while feeding.

Put up nesting boxes around the garden – they are a particularly good way to build up the local bird population, and will be used for shelter in winter and nesting in spring.

Plant plenty of berrying trees and shrubs (here, pyracantha) to attract birds to the garden in autumn and winter. Berberis, cotoneaster and *Sorbus* will also produce reliable crops of berries.

PLANNING FOR CHANGE

  !! | 1 HOUR MAX PER PROJECT ●

• **Sketching out changes over photographs of the garden is the easiest and most effective way to plan for change**
• **The simplest changes can have a major impact**

Late autumn, when the garden is relatively bare, is an excellent time to assess its overall structure and plan for change. Making a scale plan of the garden can be painstaking work, and this bird's eye view can be deceptive. Taking photographs and making changes to a 'virtual reality' garden is very much easier and more effective. So too is the use of mock-ups on the ground, which will give a very good idea of the end result. The changes can be minimal – planting a tree, for instance, or erecting trellis – and require very little work, but it is surprising what an effect they can have on the whole look and atmosphere of the garden.

TIPS

❀ If a tree is to be used for screening and privacy, siting can be crucial. To assess where it will be most effective, stand near the house and have a friend move a tall cane around the garden until the optimum planting position is established.

❀ A long central path can make an already narrow garden seem even narrower, producing a 'tunnel' effect. If sited to one side, it will give the illusion of width.

❀ For added interest in any garden, especially in winter, incorporate plenty of evergreens when planting up.

▶ *The use of flowing curves in this narrow garden makes it seem much wider, and more visually pleasing.*

1 In order to visualize what impact any changes will make, take photographs from several vantage points, including upstairs and downstairs house windows, and have them enlarged to A5 or A4 size.

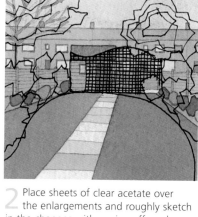

2 Place sheets of clear acetate over the enlargements and roughly sketch in the changes with a wipe-off marker pen. Those here include a tree and trellis for screening, and a reshaped lawn.

3 Once a basic plan has been decided, much of it can be double-checked by mocking up the new features on the ground. The new lawn, for example, can be indicated with a length of hosepipe.

The trellis that will screen the shed can be mocked up with canes and string, and a tall post or cane can stand in for the new tree. View them from all angles, adjusting as necessary.

DEALING WITH FALLEN LEAVES

   !!! 10 MINS PER SESSION

• **The regular collection of fallen leaves keeps the whole garden looking neat and tidy**
• **Raking up lawn leaves helps to avoid die-back of grass, the possibility of lawn diseases, and troublesome worm casts**
• **Composting leaves is a simple process and produces one of the best of all soil conditioners**

Fallen leaves, while they can look beautiful lying in drifts in lawns and borders, can be very detrimental to grass. They block out light, causing die-back, can foster lawn diseases, and they also encourage worms to come to the surface to drag the leaves down into the soil, leaving unsightly worm casts. Leaves are invaluable, however, as the source of that best of all soil conditioners – leaf mould. It is relatively high in nutrition, and its composition both retains moisture and aids drainage, making it ideal for all soils. Collecting and composting leaves takes little trouble, and works wonders for plant health and vigour when dug in or used as a mulch.

TIPS

❀ Another quick method of clearing leaves from lawns is to run a rotary mower over them with the blades set high. The leaves will be sucked up, chopped finely and collected into the grass box.

❀ Leaves are slow to break down and it can take two years for them to compost fully. Garden centres now supply biological compost activators especially for leaves, which will accelerate decomposition so that leaf mould is produced in half the time.

▶ *Make the best use of fallen leaves by collecting and composting them.*

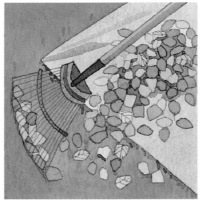
A spring-tined metal or plastic lawn rake is the most convenient way to collect leaves from a small area. To make it easier to dispose of them, rake them onto a large polythene sheet.

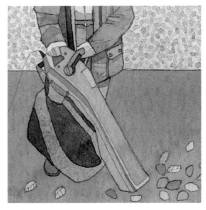
A garden vacuum makes short work of fallen leaves on larger areas. For speediest collection, set it first to blow the leaves into a heap, then simply vacuum up the whole pile.

Large quantities of leaves can be left to rot down in a simple leaf cage of strong netting supported by four stout stakes. Very small quantities can be added to the compost heap.

The other option is to store leaves in refuse sacks or old compost bags. Tie the top, make a few holes in the bag, and place in an out-of-the-way corner of the garden.

PREPARING NEW GROUND

  !!! 30 MINS PER SESSION

• **Though time-consuming, careful ground preparation saves time and trouble in future. Digging instantly improves the soil, and adding organic matter conditions it and encourages earthworm activity**
• **Good soil promotes healthy, trouble-free plants and crops**

The careful preparation of new ground – whether for kitchen beds or a new border – is hard work, but it saves a good deal of time and trouble in the long run. The simple act of digging is beneficial, relieving soil compaction and letting in air and rain. Adding organic matter improves the general condition of the earth, aids drainage on heavy soils and conserves moisture on lighter ones. It also attracts earthworms, which are vital for a healthy soil – their tunnels help aeration, and they will drag any subsequent organic mulches down into the earth. The reward for all this initial hard work is that plants grown on well-prepared, fertile soil will grow strongly and be much less vulnerable to pest and disease attack, needing an absolute minimum of care and attention.

TIPS

❀ For easier digging, wait until the ground is moist but not saturated. Pace the work so that it does not become too onerous, stopping after half an hour or so.

❀ On heavy clay soils, leave the roughly dug surface through winter. Frosts will fracture the exposed clay, making it much easier to break up into smaller pieces.

▶ *Newly turned and prepared ground makes a satisfying picture, with the promise of good things to come.*

1 Dig out a straight-sided trench approximately 30cm (1ft) wide at one end of the plot, inserting the spade to the full depth of the blade. Transfer the excavated soil to a wheelbarrow.

2 Line the base of the trench with 5–8cm (2–3in) of organic matter such as well-rotted manure or home-made compost, lightly digging it in. This will help to improve soil condition.

3 Dig a second trench, transferring the soil to the first. Break the soil up if it is heavy or compacted and remove any debris or large stones. Line with organic matter as before.

4 Continue in this way until the of the plot is reached, filling the final trench with the soil from the wheelbarrow. Unless planting immediately, leave the soil surface to 'weather' until early spring.

FROST AND SNOW PROTECTION

   !!! 5–20 MINS PER TASK

• **A series of simple frost-protection measures will keep all plants safe**
• **Removing snow from some evergreens prevents the possibility of broken branches**

Late autumn can often see the first of the wintry weather, making this a good time to start planning for protection against ground and air frosts. There is a vast range of plants that can survive harsh frosts, but it is vital to protect those on the borderline of hardiness. They take time and trouble to replace if they are killed, and some, such as shaped bays (*Laurus*), will also be very costly. Snow is only a hazard for dense-leaved evergreens, which can break under heavy snow falls; for other plants, it can provide a good insulation layer, keeping out the worst of the frosts.

TIPS

❀ Always check the hardiness of a plant before selecting a planting site. If it is slightly tender, set it in a sheltered position such as against a house wall.

❀ If you have very tender plants in the garden, they can be protected with straw and sacking in the same way as container plants (*see p.112*).

❀ Pond heaters are cheap to run, and preferable to the questionable advice of placing a pan of boiling water on the ice to melt a hole. In an icy garden, this is a potentially dangerous activity.

❀ Keep off a frosted lawn. Frozen grass will die if crushed, leaving a neat set of brown footprints.

▶ *Even in a sheltered position, slightly tender* Abutilon *'Kentish Belle' needs protection from hard frosts.*

If hard frosts are forecast, protect the crowns of less hardy plants, such as penstemon, by covering them with a cloche. Twin-walled polycarbonate cloches provide excellent insulation.

Tender evergreens, such as rosemary and bay, can be damaged or even killed by severe frost. Protect by draping with a double layer of horticultural fleece, fine netting or hessian.

Knock heavy falls of snow off dense-foliaged evergreens. If it is left to lie, the weight can break branches. Conifers are especially vulnerable, and a broken branch can ruin their symmetry.

If there are fish in the pond and ice forms, keep an area ice-free with a pond heater. If the pond ices over completely, fish can be killed by lack of oxygen and a carbon-dioxide build-up.

DIVIDING PERENNIALS

  !! 15 MINS PER CLUMP

- **Dividing plants is an easy way to increase stocks of favourite varieties**
- **It revitalizes older clumps that have died out in the middle**

Many perennial plants are clump-forming, and are easy to propagate by division. It can be beneficial too, since some can develop a lot of old, unproductive growth in the centre and begin to look unsightly. To check whether a plant is suitable for division, examine the crown (the point where the top-growth emerges). If it now has several growing points where originally there was only a single shoot, it can be divided. Some of the most popular plants can be increased in this way, including red hot pokers (*Kniphofia*), campanulas, achilleas, peonies, hostas and hardy geraniums.

■ Division can also be carried out during any mild spells through winter and early spring.

TIPS

❀ Divide garden iris in the same way as water iris (*see p.50*), planting the rhizomes so that they are only half-buried in the soil.

❀ If a plant has exceptionally dense or woody roots, divide it up with a knife, sharp spade or even a saw. Providing each portion has a good balance of healthy shoots and roots, it should grow well.

❀ Some perennials, such as hostas, can be difficult to divide while they are dormant because they die back so far that it is hard to distinguish the growing points. It is best to leave these plants until spring, when the new growth will indicate where best to make the divisions.

▶ *Congested clumps of* Kniphofia (*here, 'Little Maid') benefit from division.*

1 Using a fork, dig around and under the clump (here, *Kniphofia*), and lift it with as much root as possible. If the ground is dry before lifting, water the clump a few hours in advance.

2 Small clumps are often easy to separate by hand. Divide the clump into sections, each with a good growing tip and plenty of root, discarding unproductive material.

❀ Plant the divisions in good, well-prepared ground. Set them in at the same depth as they were originally, spreading out the roots and firming the soil around the root ball. Water well.

❀ If the roots are very congested, making it impossible to divide the clump by hand, split it up in stages with two forks back to back, using a gentle levering action to separate the roots.

TAKING HARDWOOD CUTTINGS

| | ! | 15 MINS PER 10 CUTTINGS |

• **Taking hardwood cuttings is an easy way to increase stocks of a huge range of woody plants**
• **Once inserted, cuttings can be left to root without any extra care**
• **It is a particularly good way to propagate roses, avoiding the time and trouble involved in removing suckering stems**

Taking hardwood cuttings is a very easy way to propagate a wide range of trees, shrubs and climbers, because once inserted in a trench in open, reasonably fertile ground, the cuttings need no routine care whatsoever. It is a particularly good way to obtain fresh stocks of favourite roses, since subsequent growth will be on their own roots, rather than grafted onto the vigorous rootstocks of other roses, which can throw up suckers. Taking hardwood cuttings is a method worth trying with any woody plant, since there is little to lose apart from the few minutes involved in taking the cuttings and removing any failures.

TIPS

❀ For easy, fast-rooting cuttings, select ripened stems of this year's new wood. The shoots must be healthy, with no signs of damage or disease.

❀ The use of hormone rooting powder is not essential for hardwood cuttings, but it can be used as a 'good luck' factor since it does no harm, providing it is applied only to the very base of the cutting.

❀ When taking cuttings of evergreens, such as box (*Buxus)* and privet (*Ligustrum*), remove any leaves that will be below ground level.

▶ *Bright-stemmed dogwoods* (Cornus) *are easy to propagate from hardwood cuttings.*

1 First, prepare a trench in a spare piece of ground. Insert the spade to approximately 15cm (6in), then rock it backwards and forwards to make a narrow V-shape. On heavy clay soil, line the base with coarse sand to prevent rot.

2 To take the cutting (here, *Cornus*), select a straight stem of pencil thickness. Make a sloping cut just above a leaf bud at the top, and a straight cut just below a bud at the bottom, to a length of 15–20cm (6–8in).

3 Insert the cuttings in the trench 10–15cm (4–6in) apart, so that only 2.5cm (1in) or so of stem is protruding. To create single- rather than multi-stemmed trees, set them rather deeper, so that they are just covered.

4 Firm down the soil around the cuttings and label. If there is more than one row of cuttings, space them approximately 30cm (1ft) apart. The rooted cuttings can be lifted and transplanted the following autumn.

POTTING UP LILIES

  10 MINS PER POT

- **Potting up is quick and easy**
- **Lilies are superb plants for patios, and many are highly scented**
- **Growing lilies in pots offers extra protection against the worst ravages of slugs and snails**
- **Shorter varieties are available to avoid the need for staking**

Lilies are one of the most beautiful of all flowers, and are extremely easy to grow in pots. Many are also highly perfumed, making them ideal for the patio, where the scent can be savoured at close quarters. Pot culture also makes lilies less vulnerable to slugs and snails, which can destroy plants in the open ground. To keep them going from year to year, feed fortnightly with a high-potash fertilizer while they are in full growth. Nip off the flowers when they fade, but leave the foliage to channel energy into the bulb, cutting it back when it starts to die down. Lilies can be left in the same pot for two or three years, providing you replace the top few centimetres of compost in late winter.

TIPS

❀ The keys to easy lily-growing are a well-crocked pot, free-draining compost and top-quality bulbs – they should be plump and firm, with no signs of damage or mould.

❀ To avoid having to stake lilies, choose one of the many dwarf and smaller varieties which grow to little more than 38cm (15in).

❀ Aphids on lily buds can cause damage and distort the flowers, and should be dealt with as soon as they are spotted (*see p.124*).

▶ *Lilies (here,* Lilium *'Star Gazer') add style, colour and scent to patio plantings.*

1 Using a terracotta pot (here, 25cm/10in), line the base with crocks and add a 2.5cm (1in) layer of grit, to provide extra-sharp drainage. A terracotta pot provides a more stable base than plastic, particularly for taller, top-heavy varieties.

2 Line the pot with a 5cm (2in) layer of loam-based compost and set in three bulbs, spacing them evenly. Loam-based compost gives the pot extra stability, and provides better drainage than peat-based or peat-substitute composts.

3 Top up with compost to within 2.5cm (1in) of the rim of the pot, firm down, label, and water so that the compost is moist but not saturated. Set in a sheltered position outdoors, watering only if the compost begins to dry out.

4 When growth appears in spring, set in a sunny position and insert four canes in the pot, of a length that will match the plant's eventual height. Tie the stems in regularly to protect them from wind damage and possible breakage.

FROST PROTECTION FOR CONTAINER-GROWN PLANTS

  15 MINS MAX PER PLANT

• **Simple and cost-effective frost protection measures will see all container plants safely through any harsh weather**
• **Saves the time and trouble involved in replacing affected plants**

Container-grown plants are particularly vulnerable to both ground and air frosts, and it can be upsetting to lose valued specimens, as well as costly to replace them. Evergreens are especially susceptible: if the root ball freezes, they cannot replace the water that they transpire from the leaves. Happily, there are plenty of simple measures of keeping all plants safe from frost. Wrapping the pot with insulating material prevents the root ball from freezing up, and there are several ways to protect the top-growth, depending on the degree of tenderness.

TIPS

❀ Although it may seem a kindness to bring frozen containers indoors to defrost, they should never be brought into a warm room. Rapid defrosting damages plant cells.

❀ Cluster pots together to give an extra degree of protection against frost. Smaller pots can be moved to a more sheltered position close to house walls.

❀ Winter-flowering pansies provide valuable colour in containers. A sharp frost will cause them to collapse, but they will recover fully as soon as the weather warms.

❀ Polythene sheets can be used to protect plants, but they can cause rots if left in place for too long.

▶ *Container plantings are vulnerable if the compost freezes up for long periods and so will benefit from extra protection.*

To protect the roots of container plants from freezing up, wrap the pot in bubble wrap, securing it with tape; the air trapped in the bubbles provides much better insulation than other coverings such as sacking or newspaper.

A double layer of horticultural fleece will protect slightly tender container plants such as bay (*Laurus*). Drape it loosely over the plant and secure it at the base. Sacking and fine mesh netting will also provide good protection.

Plants that are even more tender, but are too big to move under cover, need rather more protection. Bunch the leaves together if possible, pack straw around them, and keep them in place with sacking tied with string.

To give a degree of protection against ground frosts, raise pots slightly, using the terracotta 'feet' that are available from garden centres. Evenly sized stones can also be used. Raising the pot also helps to improve drainage.

CREATING RAISED VEGETABLE BEDS

  15 MINS PER SQ M/Y

• **Once the bed is created, no further digging will be necessary**
• **Annual maintenance is limited to the application of a good mulch of organic matter**

Making raised kitchen beds is an ancient technique that is enjoying renewed popularity. One of its main virtues is that once the bed is made, no further digging will be necessary. The 1.2m (4ft) width means that all work can be done from the paths, and the soil never becomes compacted. All the gardener needs to do is to top up the bed with organic matter each year to keep it fertile. The system has several other benefits. The well-structured, well-drained soil promotes strong growth; perfect growing conditions enable crops to be closely spaced, helping moisture retention and smothering weeds; and denser planting means that no food or water is wasted on 'dead' ground between rows. This dense planting can also look very attractive, especially if you plant the bed in small mixed blocks (*see p.43*).

■ Raised beds can be created at any time of year, but late autumn is ideal, allowing the soil to settle over winter.

TIPS

❀ For the best crops, site beds in an open, sunny position.

❀ If the soil is very heavy or prone to waterlogging, add plenty of gravel during the initial digging.

❀ Save space by making the paths fairly narrow – they only need to be wide enough for walking and kneeling, and 38cm (15in) is sufficient.

▶ *A raised vegetable bed allows for dense planting and high yields.*

1 Mark out an area 1.2m (4ft) wide, using pegs and string, to whatever length is available. If working on new ground, take measures to rid the site of any perennial weeds (*see p.129*), then dig it over thoroughly (*see p.107*).

2 To create an edging, use planks treated with wood preservative. Fasten them to corner pegs (also treated) and fix one or more pegs to the longer edges. Hammer the frame in so that the base of the planks is at soil level.

3 Working from the path, top up the bed with topsoil or good garden soil, then add plenty of organic matter such as well-rotted manure. Fork it in lightly so that it is incorporated into the soil, and rake level.

4 To save the labour involved in keeping paths weed-free, lay down heavy-duty permeable membrane, cutting it so that it is flush with the edge of the beds. Cover it with a layer of bark chips to protect it from wear and sunlight.

WINTER

WINTER

*The winter garden is inevitably a quiet place, but this can make whatever pleasures it offers so much more intense – stark branches made ghostly with snow, the golden flowers of winter jasmine (*Jasminum nudiflorum*), or simply the sight of newly turned ground, with its hint of good things to follow. It is a relatively relaxing time for the gardener, the main priority for early winter being to complete any outstanding plantings. Many essential tasks can be carried out at any time through the winter, while late winter is the time to prune wisteria and late-flowering clematis.*

▲ *Grasses rimed with frost make a handsome picture in the winter garden.*

SHAPING UP DECIDUOUS CLIMBERS

  !! | 25 MINS PER PLANT | ◐

• **Clearing and thinning produces more shapely plants**

Early winter is the best time to shape up deciduous non-flowering climbers because their outline is so clear and easy to assess. The actual work is easier too, because the gardener does not have to deal with a heavy hamper of leaves. Vigorous self-clinging climbers such as Virginia creepers (*Parthenocissus*) and ornamental vines (*Vitis*) will benefit from fairly rigorous thinning and pruning every few years, to give a good even cover and to remove any growth that is encroaching on doors, windows and gutters. Flowering climbers are normally pruned during the growing season, but this is a good opportunity to take out dead, overcrowded or misplaced stems and any twiggy, unproductive growth. More severe pruning will result in fewer flowers next year.

■ Non-flowering evergreen climbers are best pruned in early spring. If pruned in winter and a warm spell encourages new growth, this can be very badly damaged by frost.

1 Clear unwanted growth from house windows and doors, taking it back far enough to allow for regrowth over the next few years, and reduce drastically any growth near gutters. Self-clinging climbers (here, Virginia creeper) can be simply pulled away.

TIPS

❀ An early winter pruning date is critical for ornamental vines (forms of *Vitis*). If pruned in spring when the sap is rising, they 'bleed' profusely, and the flow of sap is hard to stem. This is potentially fatal, and will certainly weaken the plant.

❀ When pruning, always make the cut just above a bud, sloping the cut away from it so that rainwater is shed, rather than gathering at the base of the bud where it can do harm.

2 Thin out any congested growth from the rest of the plant so that it makes a good even cover. Cut the stems back to a bud that is facing in the right direction – an upward-facing bud, for instance, where there is a bare patch of wall above it.

▲ *Vigorous* Vitis vinifera *'Purpurea'.*

PRUNING LATE-FLOWERING CLEMATIS

  !!! 15–20 MINS PER 3M/10FT PLANT

- **Annual pruning is very quick and simple for this group of clematis**
- **It produces plants that are covered with flowers from top to bottom**

The pruning of late-flowering clematis is extremely simple, and while it may seem drastic, it is very effective. This group includes the large-flowered hybrids such as *Clematis* 'Perle d'Azur' and *C.* 'Ernest Markham', which are valued for their vigour and free-flowering habit from early summer to autumn. It also encompasses species clematis like *C. viticella*, *C. tangutica*, *C. florida*, and the hybrids derived from them. All these clematis flower on the current year's new growth; if left unpruned, they will commence flowering from new stems produced higher on the plant. This makes the plant look top-heavy, with the base devoid of flowers.

TIPS

❀ The topmost growth of taller varieties can be cut back in early winter if it looks untidy.

❀ Feed and mulch plants in early spring (*see p.17*) to encourage vigorous new growth. This can be surprisingly rapid, so check plants regularly through spring, tying in the new stems to make an even cover.

▲ *The long-flowering clematis 'Niobe'.*

1 In late winter, use secateurs to sever the top-growth of the clematis, removing any plant ties and disentangling it from its support.

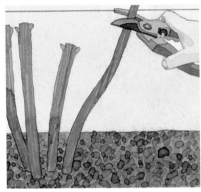

2 Now reduce the remaining main stems to approximately 30cm (1ft) above ground level, cutting just above the lowest pair of strong buds.

WISTERIA TRAINING AND PRUNING (2)

 !!! 15–20 MINS PER 3M (10FT) PLANT

- **Winter training and pruning is quick and easy**

The secondary stage of wisteria pruning (*for the first stage, see p.74*), carried out in late winter, is relatively quick because the leafless plant is so much easier to deal with.

TIPS

❀ Once the plant has filled its allotted space, winter work consists only of shortening the sideshoots and cutting back any wayward growth.

❀ Feed and mulch well in early spring (*see p.17*).

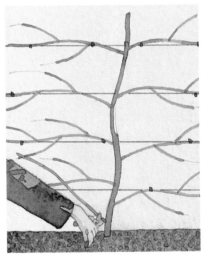

 Using secateurs, cut back the leading stem when it reaches the desired height, and prune out any new growth from the base. Cut back the new growth on horizontal branches by approximately one-third.

Further shorten the sideshoots that were pruned back in late summer (*see p.74*), taking them back to three or four buds. Always make an angled cut just above the bud. It is these sideshoots that will produce this year's flowers.

PLANTING A HEDGE

  !!! 30 MINS PER 6 PLANTS

• **Thorough preparation and good planting ensures an even, strong-growing hedge**
• **It avoids the time and trouble involved in nursing ailing plants or replanting any gaps**

A hedge – whether it is defining a boundary or simply providing shelter – is a major garden feature, and good planting is vital. A poorly planted hedge will struggle, and plants may die and leave unsightly gaps. Thorough ground preparation is essential because the plants are very tightly spaced and need the best possible start so that they grow strongly and uniformly. The precise spacing can vary from 30cm (1ft) to 60cm (2ft) or more, depending on variety, so always check the plant label when buying. After planting, keep the ground free of weeds, which will compete for water and nutrients.

■ Container-grown hedging can be planted at any time of year, but autumn is ideal, thus avoiding the necessity of frequent and time-consuming watering.

TIPS

❀ Bare-root deciduous hedging plants, available in autumn, are the most cost-effective option if a lot of plants are needed. Find a specialist supplier through the gardening press.

❀ Choose your hedging plants according to the amount of time you have to spare for trimming them. Beech (*Fagus*), for example, needs only an annual trim, while privet (*Ligustrum*) should be clipped two or three times a year.

▶ *A well-planted, well-clipped hedge provides shelter and privacy, and is the perfect backdrop for summer flowers.*

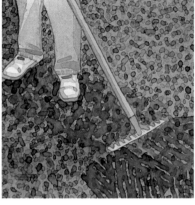
1 Dig over a wide strip of ground where the hedge is to be planted, extending a little beyond the ends. Dig to at least a spade's depth, incorporating plenty of organic matter. Level off, then apply a balanced fertilizer and lightly rake it in.

2 Water the plants well (here, privet), and mark out the line of the hedge using pegs and taut line. Make individual planting holes, then remove each plant from its pot and carefully tease out any roots that are encircling the root ball.

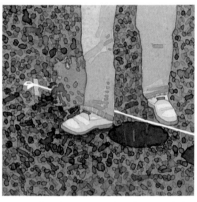
3 Set the plants in so that the top of the root ball is flush with the surrounding soil, spreading out any loosened roots. Fill in around the root-ball, taking care to avoid leaving air pockets, and firm the plant down well.

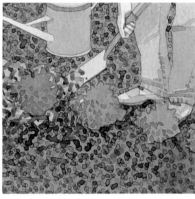
4 When all the plants are in, water well. To lock in moisture, mulch with bark chips, but make sure to keep the mulch out of direct contact with the stems. Keep well watered through any dry spells in the first spring and summer.

TRAINING NEW HEDGES

   10 MINS PER PLANT

• **Formative pruning is quick and easy, but vital for a successful hedge**
• **It encourages densely bushy growth from top to bottom of the plant, avoiding unsightly gappiness**

The training of newly planted hedges takes little time, but makes all the difference, promoting a densely bushy habit with an even cover of foliage. Some hedging plants, such as privet (*Ligustrum*) and hawthorn (*Crataegus*) will race away if not pruned back hard in their first two winters, growing into top-heavy plants with gappy growth at the base. Others, such as beech (*Fagus*) and hornbeam (*Carpinus*) are naturally bushier, so need less formative pruning. Hedging conifers need none at all; you simply have to trim the top when they reach the desired height. The only exception is yew (*Taxus*), for which training is vital. Stake it when planting, tie it in, and prune back sideshoots by half in the first winter. Thereafter, you simply need to keep the sides trimmed to encourage bushiness, cutting back the top of the hedge when it reaches the desired height.

■ For regular trimming of mature hedges, *see p.32.*

TIPS

❀ To save on ground space in smaller gardens, try to keep hedges as narrow as possible. With good initial training, there is no reason why any hedge should exceed a width of 30–60cm (1–2ft).

❀ For fast, vigorous growth of new hedges, always feed and mulch in spring (*see p.17*), and keep well watered in dry spells.

▶ *A well-trained yew hedge.*

1 After planting, reduce the height and width of vigorous plants (here, privet) by half to encourage a bushy framework. Reduce stockier shrubs, such as beech and hornbeam, by approximately one-third. Do not prune conifers, except yew.

2 In late winter of the second year, reduce the height of more vigorous, upright hedging plants, such as privet and hawthorn, by half. This may seem drastic, but is essential for a close-knit hedge. Trim the sides to a tapering shape.

3 From now on, clip plants as needed in summer, leaving the top to grow on. Trim the top back in winter to level it off and to keep it densely bushy. Once the desired height is reached, hedges need no further winter pruning.

❀ Slower-growing hedging plants, such as beech and hornbeam, need less drastic pruning in their second winter. Simply trim the top flat and cut back the main side branches and any sideshoots by approximately one-third.

PRUNING WEEPING STANDARD TREES

  !!! 10 MINS PER TREE ▶

• **Judicious pruning of weeping standard trees is quick and easy, and keeps them looking their best**

Weeping standard trees have a grace and symmetry that makes them ideal for planting as specimens so that they can be enjoyed from all angles. They look particularly good as the centrepiece in a lawn. The weeping 'head' is grafted onto a straight stem, and can be either a tree variety – such as the willow *Salix caprea* 'Kilmarnock', for example – or a shrub, such as weeping cotoneaster (*Cotoneaster salicifolius* 'Pendulus'). Pruning out unwanted growth in late winter takes very little time and is simply a matter of cutting any wayward stems that mar the overall balance of the tree. Weeping trees can also throw the occasional stem that grows vertically rather than weeping: these too should be removed.

TIPS

❀ Cut out any shoots that appear on the main stem. These are the same variety as the rootstock, rather than the grafted top-growth, and if allowed to grow on can cause the top-growth to die off.

❀ Smaller weeping standards make splendid patio specimens if grown in a large pot or tub.

▲ *Fluffy catkins of Kilmarnock willow.*

🌼 Using secateurs, cut back any wayward stems that are spoiling the overall symmetry of the tree, cutting them flush so as not to leave a stub.

🌼 Cut back any stems that are growing vertically. More may be produced through the growing season and should be cut back straight away.

REMOVING A TREE BRANCH

  !!! 5 MINS PER SMALL BRANCH ◗

• **Branch removal can revitalize congested or badly shaped trees**

If the removal of a tree branch is necessary (to relieve congestion for instance, or to shape up the tree), it is important to make a clean cut, at the right point, to minimize the possibility of infection.

TIP

❀ The branch collar can be more obvious on some trees than others. If it is difficult to identify, compromise by making the cut a short distance from the trunk.

1 Having shortened the branch to lessen its weight and reduce the risk of tearing, use a sharp pruning saw to undercut the branch by 2.5cm (1in) or so. Make the cut so that it is just outside the slight bulge of the branch collar.

2 Make the second cut by working from the top edge of the branch, just outside the branch collar as before. Saw down cleanly until the two cuts meet. There is no need to apply a wound paint to the cut area.

WINTER WASH- AND BRUSH-UP

  !!! 30 MINS PER SESSION

• **Washing out pots and trays rids them of any overwintering pests and diseases**

• **Cleaning and sharpening tools makes them more effective, and easier to use**

Winter is the ideal time for a good wash- and brush-up of garden tools and equipment, so that they are in tip-top condition well in advance of the busy spring months. Washing down pots and trays is simple work, and removes the dirt that could be harbouring pests and diseases. Tools are much easier to use when cleaned and sharpened, and look so much better, while the mower (if not sent for service) will benefit from a quick and easy clean-up.

TIPS

❀ Cleaning the outside of ornamental terracotta pots is counter-productive, removing the mellow patina that they acquire with age and which adds to their charm.

❀ Revive wooden handles with a coat of linseed oil, rubbing it in well.

❀ Stainless steel tools cut out the need for cleaning and sharpening.

❀ Each year, wooden tubs should be treated with a wood preservative that is not toxic to plants. If the tub has been emptied completely, this is a good opportunity to treat the inside as well as the outside to prolong its life (clean the inside before applying).

❀ Metal wheelbarrows also need a little care. Rub down any rusty parts with a stiff wire brush or emery paper and prevent recurrence by applying a metal protection paint, formulated for outdoor use to affected areas.

▶ *A quick overhaul of tools and equipment brings order to the garden shed.*

❀ Wash pots and trays in a bucket of hot, soapy water, using a stiff brush to remove any dirt that may be harbouring pests or diseases. Larger pots and tubs that are too heavy to move can be cleaned *in situ*, then hosed down to remove any loosened dirt.

❀ Clean any dirt off hand tools as for pots and trays and leave to dry. To create a smoother surface that will make for easier digging, rub down any rusty areas with a wire brush. Finally, spray the tools with an oil-based lubricant, rubbing it in thoroughly with a cloth.

❀ Clean any dried grass clippings from the underside and blades of lawnmowers, using a stiff wire brush. Clean the whole machine with a damp cloth, then rub down any rust on metal parts and spray with an oil-based lubricant. Store mowers in dry conditions.

❀ Sharpen the cutting edge of hoes and spades to improve their cutting ability. When well sharpened, they are much more effective, and easier to use. First clean them off as above, then clamp them in a vice. Using a fine, flat metal file, hone the leading (upper) edge.

CARING FOR GARDEN FURNITURE

  !!! 10–45 MINS

- **A little annual care keeps garden furniture looking good**
- **Applying teak oil restores the colour of hardwood and prolongs the life of softwood furniture**

Garden furniture can be very expensive, so a little annual care makes sense financially, and keeps it looking good. Hardwood furniture will last indefinitely without any special treatment, but some gardeners like to restore the colour using teak oil. Softwood furniture is not so durable, and an annual application of teak oil will help to prolong its life. Rust on metal furniture is relatively rare, particularly if any knocks or chips are painted over straight away, but if it does get a hold, it is a quick and easy job to remove it and repaint.

TIPS

❀ Store tubular metal furniture under cover when not in use. The rivets of the folding parts may rust.

❀ Softwoods are sometimes varnished to protect them from the weather. Check them over for any cracking or splitting, rubbing down affected areas and re-varnishing with heavy-duty yacht varnish.

❀ For an instant new look for ornate metal furniture, simply spray it with car paint in your chosen colour.

❀ Softwood furniture can be treated with wood preservative instead of teak oil. To protect the base of the legs, which are the most vulnerable to rotting, stand them in cans filled with preservative for 24 hours.

❀ When painting or repainting wooden garden furniture, always use a microporous paint to prevent rot.

▶ *Good furniture is well worth looking after.*

To restore the colour of hardwood furniture, and prolong the life of softwood, treat with teak oil. Use a stiff brush to dislodge any dirt or algal growth, then wash with warm, soapy water. When dry, oil lightly with a soft, absorbent cloth.

Remove any dirt from plastic and synthetic resin furniture simply by wiping it down with a cloth dipped in hot, soapy water. On dimpled surfaces, more ingrained dirt can be removed by using a non-scouring cleanser.

1 To remove rust from metal garden furniture, first brush off any loose flakes using a stiff wire brush or treat with a rust-dissolving jelly available from car accessory dealers, then rub down the area with wire wool.

2 Paint over the cleaned area using an outdoor grade metal paint, working it into any intricately cast areas to provide an even cover. To obtain a good colour match, use a small pot of touch-up paint available from car accessory shops.

PRUNING APPLE AND PEAR TREES

  !!! 45 MINS PER MATURE TREE

• **Careful pruning in the early years creates a balanced, shapely tree**
• **Routine annual pruning stimulates the production of fruit and opens out the tree to let in light and air, making it less vulnerable to pests and diseases**

The formative pruning of apple and pear trees is important, to create a shapely, well-balanced framework. Once this is established, annual pruning consists mainly of cutting back sideshoots from the main stems to induce fruiting or, for tip-bearing apples, cutting out a proportion of the older wood to promote new fruiting wood. At the same time, it is important to cut out any congested or crossing growth in the centre of the tree, to form a goblet shape, so that all growth receives its fair share of sun and air and remains healthy and more resistant to pest and disease attack.

TIPS

❀ If the tree was bought as a 'whip' (a young, unbranched tree), induce branching by cutting it back in its first winter to approximately 75cm (30in), just above a bud.

❀ Secateurs are fine for pruning young fruit trees. As trees mature, loppers make light work of removing any older, thicker wood.

❀ The relatively new, single-stemmed fruit trees, supplied under a variety of brand names, need no pruning at all. The fruit is produced on short spurs from the main stem. They are ideal for the smaller garden, or for growing in patio tubs.

▶ *Careful training and pruning promote an open, shapely growth habit for apple and pear trees, as well as a good yield.*

1 In the first winter, prune out the leading stem, leaving three or four strong branches that will form the framework of the tree. Shorten the remaining branches by half, cutting just above an outward-facing bud.

2 In the second winter, cut back all vigorous new growth by half, above an outward-facing bud, to encourage more branching framework growth. At the same time, prune back sideshoots in the crown of the tree to four buds.

3 In the third and subsequent years, prune back all new growth on the outermost stems by approximately one-third, cut back young sideshoots to five or six buds to form fruiting spurs, and cut back any congested or crossing stems.

❀ Some apple trees bear their fruit at the tips of the branches, including popular varieties such as 'Bramley's Seedling'. Once the main framework has been established, restrict pruning to removing some of the older, fruited wood.

THE HEALTHY GARDEN

Even the best-regulated garden can have its fair share of problems, but there are many ways to cut down the time spent on them. Soil improvement together with good planting are vital – a happy, vigorous plant is more resistant to pest and diseases. Vigilance is equally important, because prompt action in the early stages will save trouble later on, whatever the problem. Of the many control methods, chemicals are the fiercest and should be used sparingly. Always follow the manufacturer's instructions, never mix chemicals, store them away from children and pets, and dispose of them safely.

▲ Aphids can distort the buds and flowers of roses and many other plants.

APHIDS

 !!! 10–15 MINS PER SESSION

• **Spraying provides good aphid control, but encouraging predators, such as lacewings, can be an even more effective method**

Sap-feeding aphids are one of the commonest of garden pests, and they can vary in colour from green, through yellow, pink and brown to black. They attack an enormous range of plants, weakening them by sucking the sap, causing distorted growth of flowers and shoots, and transmitting viruses from plant to plant. The sticky 'honeydew' that they excrete creates the secondary problem of sooty mould in the same way as scale insects (*see p.127*). Organic or chemical sprays will kill them, but the simplest and easiest solution is to let nature do the work for you by encouraging predators. One lacewing larva, for example, can consume three hundred aphids. A lacewing chamber, filled with straw impregnated with pheromone attractant, will ensure a garden population. Birds, too, will eat any amount of aphids, so it is wise to make them feel at home (*see p.104*).

 The simplest and quickest way to get rid of aphid colonies on sturdy stems and leaves is to squash them by running a gloved hand over them. On fragile plants, dab them off with a tissue.

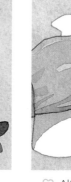

Alternatively, spray the surface and underside of leaves with a soap-based insecticide. If using a chemical insecticide, use one that does not harm beneficial insects such as ladybirds.

TIPS

❀ Woolly aphids, most commonly seen on apple trees, hide under a grey/white fluffy coating, which makes it difficult to spray them effectively. The simplest way to get rid of them is to wash them off the tree with a strong jet from the garden hose.

❀ A lacewing chamber guarantees a high population of aphid-eating insects. Another good way to attract lacewings, which feed on nectar as well as aphids, is to grow the poached egg plant (*Limnanthes douglasii*), which is particularly rich in nectar. This annual is very easily raised from seed (*see p.21*).

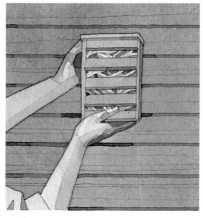

Adult lacewings and their larvae are voracious predators of aphids. To ensure a good population, hang up a special lacewing chamber in spring and transfer it to a garage or shed in autumn.

SLUGS AND SNAILS

   !!! 5–10 MINS PER SESSION

- **There are many easy ways to keep down the slug and snail population**
- **Slug pellets work well, but should be used with care**
- **Organic and biological controls can be very effective**

Of all garden pests, slugs and snails, with their characteristic silvery trail of dried slime, are probably the most distressing. They can devastate seedling crops, make serious inroads into more mature crops, and turn the leaves of some ornamental plants, particularly hostas, into a lacework pattern of holes. They are so widespread that they can never be entirely eliminated, but several control measures will help to minimize the damage they cause.

Slug pellets work extremely well on both slugs and snails, but many gardeners are wary of using them because they are so toxic, both to children and pets, who may accidentally eat them, and to the birds and hedgehogs that may prey on poisoned corpses. If you do use them, scatter them thinly, since they are only effective for two or three days and will need to be replaced.

Organic measures, such as encircling plants with gravel or setting beer traps, can be almost as effective as chemicals, and rather kinder on the environment.

Biological control, using parasitic nematodes, seem to be the most effective of all against slugs, and though very expensive, are well worth considering as protection for young crops in the kitchen garden. Keeping weeds down is important too. Slugs like to rest in cool, damp spots, and a neglected, weedy patch provides perfect conditions.

TIPS

❋ Mulching with a layer of cocoa-shell or eggshells can be a very effective deterrent against slugs and snails, especially for young bedding plants. The brittle edges make a sharp surface and this will discourage them from going any further.

❋ Plastic bottles, sliced off at the top and bottom and placed over seedlings, will provide some protection from slugs and snails. They will not, however, protect them from ground-dwelling species of slug.

❋ Night-time patrols can net good catches of slugs, which are most active in the evening, especially in warm, damp weather. Whole platoons can be found on the lawn, for instance. The simplest way to dispose of them is to drop them into a bucket of heavily salted water.

❋ Empty out beer traps into the compost heap. It is some consolation to know that the creatures that have been destroying plants will in future be helping to feed them.

🌼 Scatter slug pellets thinly around plants, spacing them 10–15cm (4–6in) apart. They are highly toxic, and if children or pets use the garden, it is a wise precaution to conceal them so that they are not accidentally eaten.

🌼 Circle plants with a barrier of gravel, ashes, crushed eggshells or thorny cuttings. Slugs and snails find the abrasive surface uncomfortable, and will not cross it. The mulch will eventually weather down and need to be replaced.

🌼 Sink a jar or plastic cup just proud of the soil and half fill with beer. Slugs and snails climb into the jar, become too inebriated to climb out, and drown. In the vegetable garden, set jars at regular 90cm (3ft) intervals.

🌼 Water microscopic nematodes onto the soil at the prescribed dilution rate. These parasites infect slugs and are especially useful for destroying ground-dwelling slugs, which are difficult to deal with by any other method.

VINE WEEVILS

 !!! 10 MINS PER SESSION ▶

- **Checking the compost of newly-bought plants helps to reduce the damage done by vine weevil larvae**
- **Adult weevils are so slow-moving that they are easy to destroy without resorting to chemicals**
- **Biological control is very effective**

Vine weevils are one of the worst of insect pests because they are so insidious. The adults do little damage, confining themselves to eating notches out of leaves, but the larvae are much more destructive. These pests attack a wide range of plants, but are particularly fond of the soft succulent roots of bedding plants. Once rootless, there is no hope of reviving them. Vigilance is one of the best ways of keeping down weevil numbers – checking the compost of newly bought bedding plants, and looking out for adult weevils around the garden. Biological control (microscopic nematodes watered onto the soil) works well, but is very temperature-sensitive, which limits the times when it can be applied.

TIPS

❀ Apply a barrier of non-drying glue (available from garden centres) around the rim of individual pots to provide short-term protection against weevils. It will have to be reapplied when the inevitable build-up of trapped insects and debris renders it ineffective.

❀ If you are happy to use chemical pesticides, there is now a plant-protection compost containing an insecticide that kills vine weevil larvae, as well as any pests feeding on the top-growth. It is not, however, suitable for edible plants.

▶ *Gold speckling distinguishes the vine weevil from other weevils.*

1 To check for the presence of vine weevil larvae, inspect the root balls of bedding plants. The larvae are sometimes visible on the outer part of the root ball and are very distinctive: approximately 1cm (½in) long, plump and off-white with a brown head.

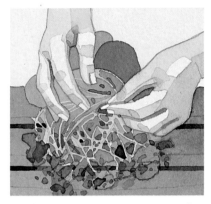

2 If weevil larvae are present, you will need to dismantle the whole root ball. Water the plant first, to make the roots more pliable, then lay it down and carefully tease the compost away from the roots, trying to minimize any damage. Remove and destroy any larvae.

❀ If weevil larvae are a permanent problem in pots and tubs, the most effective treatment is a biological control such as microscopic nematodes, which infect the larvae with lethal bacteria. Mix them in the watering can and water them into pots in spring and late summer.

❀ The other way to keep down the weevil population is to look out for the adults: they are slow-moving, approximately 1cm (½in) long, and grey-black with a fine gold speckling; they are most active at dusk. The simplest way to eradicate them is to squash them.

SCALE INSECTS AND SOOTY MOULD

 !!! 10–15 MINUTES PER PLANT

• **Scale insects can seriously weaken plants unless dealt with early on**

Scale insects, feeding on stems and the underside of leaves, are easily overlooked until tell-tale sooty mould begins to form. This is a fungus that colonizes the sticky 'honeydew' excreted by the scale insects. The insects themselves are limpet-like, hidden under the protective rounded or oval, white, yellow or brown shell. Some scale insects are specific to certain plants, but others are less specialized and will attack a wide range. Brown scale (dark brown, oval and up to 5mm/¼in long) feeds on numerous garden plants including magnolias, cotoneasters, roses and wisteria. Small plants are relatively easy to treat, by removing affected leaves or spraying, but control of scale on larger plants can be difficult.

▲ *Soft scale insect on a bay leaf.*

TIPS

❀ Sprays are most effective in early summer and midsummer, when the newly hatched 'nymphs' are active, looking for a place to settle and feed.

❀ A winter tar oil wash can be effective for deciduous trees and shrubs. They must be fully dormant, and it is vital to protect any evergreen plants in the area from the toxic spray.

Use a proprietary spray two or three times, at fortnightly intervals, between late spring and early autumn. If a few leaves are affected, pick them off.

If sooty mould has formed, remove it by wiping down the leaves of smaller plants with a damp cloth. Larger plants can be hosed down.

LEAF SPOTS AND RUSTS

 !!! 5 MINS PER PLANT

• **Leaf spots and rusts can weaken plants, so prompt action is essential**

Leaf spots (normally black or brown) and rusts (an orange/brown speckling on the underside of leaves) are caused by any number of fungal infections. Rose black spot is one of the commonest. Serious attacks can defoliate plants. It is vital to catch them at an early stage.

TIP

❀ Select resistant varieties where possible, and choose fungicides tailored to the plant type.

If only a few leaves are affected, pick them off the plant and destroy any infected material. More serious cases of leaf spot or rust can be sprayed with Bordeaux mixture, or with an appropriate chemical fungicide.

To minimize the possibility of attack from leaf spot or rust, feed plants with a high-potash fertilizer in spring (*see p.17*), and spray with fungicide as they come into leaf in spring, repeating the treatment if necessary.

DOWNY AND POWDERY MILDEWS

  !!! 5–10 MINS PER PLANT

• **Downy and powdery mildews are unsightly and very debilitating, so early treatment is essential**
• **Removing affected material often controls minor outbreaks, but spraying may become necessary**

Mildews are disfiguring, and can seriously weaken plants. Downy mildew attacks a wide range of plants and is most prevalent during long wet spells. It produces a greyish white coating on the underside of leaves, with a yellowing of the upper surface. Densely grown plants and crops, especially on a poorly drained soil, are most at risk.

Powdery mildew also affects many plants, notably roses and Michaelmas daisies (*Aster*). The powdery white coating, normally on the upper surfaces of leaves, can also extend to stems and buds. It thrives in hot, dry weather and is often at its worst in autumn after a hot summer.

For both these mildews, removing affected leaves at the first sign of attack can sometimes solve the problem, but spraying may become inevitable. Improving the growing conditions for both border and container plants will also help.

TIPS

✿ To help prevent mildew in container plants, mix water-retaining crystals with the compost before planting up the pots.

✿ Where possible, buy resistant varieties – some roses, for instance, are much less prone to powdery mildew than others.

▶ *Roses are especially prone to powdery mildew, which can affect the stems and buds as well as the leaves.*

The simplest way to deal with downy mildew is to cut out and destroy any affected material at the first sign of attack, then spray the remainder with organic Bordeaux mixture or a specially formulated chemical fungicide.

To avoid the problem in future, improve the drainage of heavy garden soils by digging in plenty of grit or gravel before planting. In summer bedding containers, provide extra-sharp drainage using a layer of crocks (*see p.52*).

Treat any attack of powdery mildew in the same way as you would downy mildew, by first removing all affected material. Spray the remainder with an appropriate organic or chemical fungicide, respraying if the problem recurs.

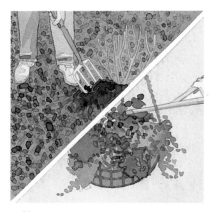

The best way to avoid powdery mildew in the garden is to mulch plants when the soil is moist (*see p.17*), so that the moisture is locked in. Container-grown bedding plants should be kept regularly well watered.

WEED-INFESTED SITES

🕷 !!! 1 HOUR PER 10 SQ M/YD ●

• The two-step method of weed clearance is relatively quick and very effective

Neglected areas that have become thoroughly weed-infested are very tiring and time-consuming to clear by digging, particularly if there are a lot of deep-rooted perennial weeds. If you do not object to the use of chemicals, the easiest method is to cut down the weeds in spring, then spray with glyphosate weedkiller in midsummer when growth is at its lushest and most vulnerable. Glyphosate is one of the more useful weedkillers, since it is harmless once dry and does not persist in the soil, so that the site can be planted up straight away. If you prefer to clear by digging, be sure to remove all the roots of perennials such as bindweed (*Convolvulus*), which can resprout from any overlooked portion.

▲ *Bindweed is a highly persistent weed.*

TIPS

❀ Apply weedkiller on a still day, to prevent the spray from drifting onto cultivated plants.

❀ A rotavator is counter-productive on weed-infested land because it chops up and distributes the roots of perennial weeds. It is, however, the quickest way to turn over the ground once the site has been cleared.

1 To clear a site that is completely overgrown, cut back any woody weeds, such as brambles, to encourage lush spring growth. A brushcutter makes quick work of even the toughest weeds.

2 When weeds are at their most vigorous in midsummer, spray them with a glyphosate weedkiller. A knapsack sprayer saves time on larger areas. Wait for 4–5 weeks and spray any regrowth.

ANNUAL WEEDS

🕷 !!! 1–5 MINS PER SQ M/YD

• Hoeing and hand-pulling annual weeds is quick and easy work

Annual weeds are easy to get rid of simply by hoeing or by pulling them up by hand, but it is best to do this before they have set seed or you may find that you have to do the job all over again. In hot, dry weather, the weeds can be left on the soil to wither.

TIP

❀ Mulches will suppress annual weeds completely (*see p.17*). Cocoa shell, which deters slugs, is very useful for young border plants and crops

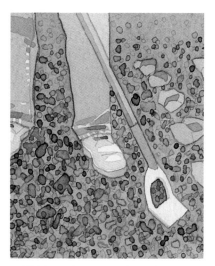
 The easiest way to keep down annual weeds is to hoe them out as soon as they emerge, slicing them off just below soil level. Hoeing when the soil is dry is the most effective method, since some weeds can re-root into moist soil.

More mature annual weeds are easy to pull out by hand, particularly when the soil is moist. If they are flowering or have set seed, bag them up and dispose of them, rather than adding them to the compost heap.

PERENNIAL WEEDS

  !!! 5 MINS PER PLANT

• Digging can eradicate shallow-rooted perennial weeds such as perennial stinging nettles
• Weedkiller is the easiest solution for deep-rooted weeds
• Mulches will help to suppress a number of perennial weeds

Perennial weeds use all kinds of survival tactics, quite apart from spreading by seed. Some, such as dandelion and dock, have deep tap-roots that are difficult to dig out, and will regrow from any small piece left behind. Bindweed will also resprout from its wide-spreading, deep roots, and is extremely difficult to dig out. Horsetail and knotweed are so deep-rooted (to 2m/6ft or more) that digging is ineffective. Brambles root where the stem tips touch the ground, and ground elder sends up stems from creeping roots. Mulching will help to smother less vigorous perennials, such as perennial nettle and and willow herb, but the easiest solution for all perennials is to use glyphosate weedkiller, which is harmless when dry and does not persist in the soil. Where cultivated plants are growing close by, paint it on the foliage, rather than spraying.

TIPS

❀ If weeds are creeping in from a neighbouring garden, a physical barrier such as thick polythene, set vertically in the ground to 45cm (18in) or so, is a good deterrent.

❀ One of the most successful and simplest methods of deterring perennial weeds is to plant plenty of ground-cover plants such as hostas and hardy geraniums.

▶ *Perennial weeds can swamp garden plants if not controlled.*

Some perennial weeds (here, creeping buttercup) are relatively shallow-rooted and are easy to lift with a hand fork. If they have spread into a large clump, it can be quicker to lift the clump with a garden fork.

A thick mulch of bark or organic matter (*see p.17*) helps to smother perennial weeds. Some will penetrate the mulch, and many will then root into this looser layer. This makes them much easier to remove simply by hand-pulling.

Deep-rooted weeds, such as bindweed, are difficult to eradicate by digging. It is much quicker and easier to use glyphosate weedkiller, painting it onto the leaves rather than spraying if there are cultivated plants nearby.

To eradicate horsetail (*above*) and Japanese knotweed, wait until they are growing strongly in midsummer, then crush the stems before spraying with weedkiller. It can take two or three seasons to destroy them.

LAWN WEEDS

 !!! 20 MINS PER SMALL LAWN ◐

- **There are many simple measures that will control lawn weeds**
- **Looking after the grass is the most effective weed control of all, since it simply smothers them**

Weeds are inevitable in any lawn. The most harmful are those such as dandelions and plantains that form a ground-hugging rosette of leaves and shade out a whole circle of grass. The three basic control measures are hand-weeding, spot-treating with weedkiller, and the use of soluble or granular weedkillers over the whole lawn. The long-term solution, however, is to encourage vigorous, healthy grass growth which will smother seedling weeds and solve the problem for you. Feeding in spring and autumn (*see p.55*) will encourage strong, dense growth. Dealing with humps in the lawn (*see p.40*) will also help, by preventing the bald patches where the grass is scalped by the mower, which are rapidly colonized by weeds. Raking the lawn before mowing can help to control the spread of creeping weeds such as trefoil, by placing them in the path of the mower blades.

 ## TIPS

✿ Try to cultivate a relaxed attitude about weeds in lawns. Some, like daisies, are very pretty and are not too invasive, and others, such as clover, have the virtue of staying green during a drought.

✿ If the lawn is very badly weed-infested and growing poorly, it may be simpler, in the long run, to dig it up and start all over again with new turf (*see pp.38–39*) or from seed (*see p.87*).

▶ *Lawn weeds are often unsightly and detrimental to the vigour of the grass.*

✿ Use a pronged daisy grubber to lift shallow-rooted weeds such as plantain. Insert it under the plant and gently rock it back and forth to loosen the roots. Do this when the soil is moist, so that the roots come away easily.

✿ A long-handled weeding tool is useful if there are a lot of weeds to eradicate. Some are claw-shaped, others lift out the weed and eject it using a built-in plunger. For easy disposal, collect up the weeds on a polythene sheet.

✿ Treat deeper-rooted weeds, such as dandelion, which are hard to dig out without disturbing the turf, with a spot-weeder formulated for lawn use, which kills the weeds but not the grass. It is useful for border weeds too.

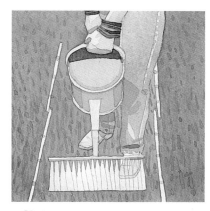

✿ If the lawn is badly infested, treat with a liquid or granular weedkiller. A can with a dribble bar is the easiest way to apply liquid weedkiller. A combined weed, feed and moss-killer, applied in late spring, is also effective.

AN A–Z DIRECTORY OF EASY-CARE PLANTS

The plants featured here were chosen on three criteria – ease of growth, a long period of interest, and last but by no means least, sheer beauty. Most of the plants will thrive in all types of soil, so long as it is reasonably fertile and well-drained. If they have any special requirement (an acid soil, for example), this is always mentioned under the plant entry. The 'star' symbols pick out the best and easiest of a wonderful bunch.

Allium giganteum

KEY TO SYMBOLS
☆ star plants   H height
○ full sun   S spread
◑ partial shade   ✀ pruning
● shade   ✂ propagation

ACER (Maple)
A splendidly varied family of trees and shrubs, renowned for the brilliant autumn colour of the deciduous varieties. Shrubby *A.* 'Garnet' is one of the best of the Japanese maples, forming a mound of finely cut red-purple foliage. The paper-bark maple, *A. griseum*, is a slow-growing tree, the shaggy orange-brown bark providing year-round interest. The snake-bark maple, *A. pensylvanicum*, is equally striking, with large, lobed green leaves that turn yellow in autumn, and striking green and white striped bark. All of the above are deciduous and thrive in a cool, moist soil.
○◑ Shrubs: H 1.2–3m (4–10ft), S 1–4m (3–12ft). Trees: H 8–12m (25–40ft), S 10–12m (30–40ft)
✀ None
✂ Seed sown outdoors in mid-autumn

ACHILLEA (Yarrow)
Tough and trouble-free, achilleas are one of the easiest of border perennials, producing large plates of flowers above feathery foliage over a long period in summer and early autumn. Although most are fairly tall, the sturdy stems do not require staking. Two deservedly popular varieties are the stately evergreen *A. filipendulina* 'Gold Plate', with bright yellow flowerheads, and the more compact *A.* 'Moonshine', with evergreen, lance-shaped leaves and light yellow flowerheads.
○ H 15cm–1.2m (6in–4ft), S 23–60cm (9in–2ft)
✀ Cut hard back in late autumn
✂ Division in early spring or late autumn

ALLIUM (Ornamental onion)
Easy, reliable bulbs for late spring and early summer colour. *A. cristophii* produces glittering purple globes of flowers up to 20cm (8in) across, while the towering *A. giganteum* produces smaller, more densely packed deep lilac globes.
○ H 30cm–1.2m (1–4ft), S 5–15cm (2–6in) per bulb
✀ Remove faded flowers
✂ Bulbs planted in autumn, self-sown seeds

AMELANCHIER
(Juneberry, snowy mespilus) ☆
A. lamarckii is a valuable deciduous small tree or shrub, providing a long season of interest – bronzy young foliage, white spring blossom, edible fruit that ripens in a good summer, and wonderful autumn leaf colour. Grows well on any soil, except chalk, provided it is not bone dry.
○◑ H and S 3m (10ft) or more
✀ None
✂ Ripened seed sown outdoors in summer, semi-ripe cuttings in midsummer

ASPLENIUM (Spleenwort)
The glossy, evergreen fronds of *A. scolopendrium* are long, narrow and undivided. *A.s.* 'Crispum' is one of the prettiest cultivars, with heavily waved leaf margins. Aspleniums need a humus-rich, moist but not waterlogged soil.
◑ H to 60cm (2ft), S 60cm (2ft)
✀ None
✂ Division in spring

BERBERIS (Barberry)
A fine group of tough shrubs, which are particularly striking in the coloured-foliage forms. Deciduous *B. thunbergii* 'Bagatelle' and 'Dart's Red Lady' are very compact, forming mounded, red-purple domes. 'Rose Glow' is rather taller, with pink-purple white-flecked leaves on arching stems, and makes a good informal hedging plant.
○◑ H 30cm–1.5m (1–5ft), S 30cm–1.2m (1–4ft)
✀ None
✂ Semi-ripe cuttings in midsummer

BETULA (Birch)
Quick-growing deciduous trees valued for their graceful, open habit, attractive spring catkins and for the year-round interest provided by the many white-barked varieties. *B. utilis* var. *jacquemontii* is one of the best of the upright varieties and ghostly 'Silver Shadow' is outstanding, *B. pendula* 'Youngii' is a smaller weeping tree that makes a superb lawn specimen.
○◑ H 6–11m (20–35ft), S 6m (20ft)
✀ None
✂ Seed sown outdoors in autumn

BUDDLEJA ☆
B. davidii (butterfly bush) is a vigorous, deciduous, indestructible shrub, especially useful in a hot, dry spot and in poor soils. The arching stems are tipped with long cones of flowers from midsummer to mid-autumn, in a wide range of colours – deep purple 'Black Knight' is very striking.
○ H 3m (10ft), S 5m (15ft)
✀ Cut hard back in early spring.
✂ Semi-ripe cuttings and cuttings in water in midsummer, hardwood cuttings in late autumn

Berberis thunbergii

Clematis 'Bill MacKenzie'

Cotoneaster horizontalis

CALLUNA (Heather, ling)

Good evergreen ground-cover plants, flowering from summer to autumn in a range of white and pink shades. Those with coloured foliage (anything from bronze to silver and gold) such as 'Gold Haze' and coppery 'Multicolor' are especially useful for winter interest. Must have an acid soil.

○ H 15–60cm (6in–2ft), S 30–60cm (1–2ft)

✄ Trim over in spring

↬ Semi-ripe cuttings in midsummer

CAMELLIA

Camellias are evergreen, and the most glamorous of all spring-flowering shrubs for a lime-free soil. Forms of *C. williamsii* such as pink 'Donation' are the hardiest, but all camellias need shelter from wind and severe frost, in a south- or west-facing position. Protect through any prolonged frosts.

○◑ H and S 2–2.5m (6–8ft)

✄ To shape plants if necessary

↬ Semi-ripe cuttings in midsummer

CEANOTHUS

Evergreen *C.* 'Autumnal Blue' is the most vigorous of all these attractive wall shrubs, forming a dense, weed-suppressing canopy. It flowers midsummer to autumn. Mound-forming *C. thyrsiflorus* var. *repens* makes excellent groundcover. Grow all ceanothus in a sheltered site.

○ H 1–3m (3–10ft), S 2.5–3m (8–10ft)

✄ Trim lightly in mid-spring to encourage dense leaf cover

↬ Semi-ripe cuttings in mid- to late summer

CHOISYA (Mexican orange blossom) ☆

A fine group of aromatic, glossy-leaved evergreen shrubs with orange-blossom-scented flowers in late spring, followed by further small flushes through to autumn. Golden-leaved *C. ternata* 'Sundance' produces fewer flowers, and colours best in sun. Very reliable and easy.

○◑ H and S 2m (6ft)

✄ To tidy the plant if necessary

↬ Semi-ripe cuttings in midsummer

CLEMATIS

The best value clematis are those that flower continuously from early summer through to early autumn. This group includes the popular 'Ernest Markham' and 'Perle d'Azur'. 'Bill MacKenzie', flowering from midsummer to late autumn, is valued for its orange, bell-shaped flowers. Always plant clematis deeply (*see p.92*), to avoid clematis wilt, in a position where the roots are shaded.

○◑ H 3m (10ft), S 1m (3ft)

✄ Cut back early clematis in early summer (*see p.59*), and late-flowering clematis hard in late winter (*see p.117*)

↬ Semi-ripe cuttings in midsummer, layering spring

CORNUS (Dogwood) ☆

The dogwoods grown for their coloured bark are extremely attractive in winter, forming bristling stands of shiny stems in shades of red, green and yellow. Tough and easy, they are excellent plants, although *C. stolonifera* 'Flaviramea' can be invasive. Red-stemmed *C. alba* 'Elegantissima' has the bonus of white-variegated leaves in summer.

○◑ H and S 3m (10ft)

✄ Cut hard back in early spring (*see p.20*)

↬ Semi-ripe cuttings in midsummer, hardwood cuttings in late autumn, layering in early spring.

COTINUS (Smoke bush)

The large, wispy sprays of tiny flowers give cotinus its common name of smoke bush. It is an easy, undemanding deciduous shrub, with some lovely foliage colours from wine red to deep purple – *C. coggygria* 'Royal Purple' is outstanding. All varieties colour up beautifully in autumn.

○ H and S 2.5m (8ft) or more

✄ None required, but can be pruned hard for larger leaves

↬ Layering in early spring

COTONEASTER

An easy, useful group of evergreen and deciduous shrubs, producing small flowers followed by long-lasting berries. They range from prostrate plants good for groundcover, through wall shrubs such as the herringbone *C. horizontalis*, to large bushes that can be used for hedging and screening. Tolerant of poor conditions.

○◑ H 8cm–5m (3in–15ft), S 60cm–4m (2–12ft)

✄ Trim hedges and formal wall-trained plants to shape in late summer, retaining as many berries as possible

↬ Semi-ripe cuttings in mid- to late summer, layering in early spring

ELAEAGNUS

Evergreen forms of elaeagnus provide some extremely bright variegations, making them particularly useful shrubs for shady positions. One of the boldest is *E. pungens* 'Maculata', the dark green leaves heavily splashed with gold. A good, unfussy plant and very tolerant of coastal winds and dry soil.

○◑ H and S 2–5m (6–15ft)

✄ To tidy the plant if necessary, and to

Elaeagnus pungens 'Maculata'

Euphorbia characias subsp. *wulfenii*

Geranium wallichianum 'Buxton's Variety'

remove any shoots that have reverted to plain green
✿ Semi-ripe cuttings in midsummer

ERICA (Heath)

Winter-flowering *E. carnea* makes useful, reliable evergreen ground cover, as well as a colourful infill when planting containers in autumn. Semi-trailing *E. carnea* 'Springwood White' is especially pretty, and many cultivars have bronze or gold foliage that adds interest to the summer garden. *E. carnea* grows in any soil, including chalk.
○ H 15cm (6in), S 25–45cm (10–18in)
✂ Trim over in spring
✿ Semi-ripe cuttings in mid- to late summer

EUONYMUS

Tough, trouble-free and tolerant of poor soil, evergreen *E. fortunei* is shapely and compact, with many white- and gold-variegated forms such as 'Silver Queen' and 'Emerald 'n' Gold'. Invaluable shrubs for any garden, most are ground-hugging, others form mounded domes, and all will start to climb, if planted against a wall. Dome-shaped forms make good clipped specimens.
○ ◑ H 30cm–1m (1–3ft), S 45cm–1.5m (18in–5ft)
✂ Clip specimen plants in mid-spring and midsummer
✿ Semi-ripe cuttings in midsummer

EUPHORBIA (Spurge)

A superb perennial with a strong architectural habit. *E. characias* subsp. *wulfenii* has stately bottle-brush stems, furnished with grey-green leaves and topped by huge domes of long-lasting, yellow-green flowers. *E. amygdaloides* var. *robbiae* is deeper green and a useful colonizer of dry shade under trees. Both are evergreen.

○ ◑ H 60cm–1.2m (2–4ft), S 1.2m (4ft) or more
✂ Cut out stems when flowers fade (take care: the sap is a severe irritant)
✿ Division in early to mid-spring

GERANIUM (Cranesbill) ☆

Hardy geraniums are splendid ground-cover plants, the tough rootstock and densely mounded canopy of leaves smothering all weeds. They are undemanding, and the small flowers are produced in profusion, often over a very long period. *G. wallichianum* 'Buxton's Variety' (syn. 'Buxton's Blue'), with its white centred saucer flowers, is especially charming. They self-seed readily, but unwanted seedlings are easy to remove.
○ ◑ H 15cm–1.2m (6in–4ft), S 30cm–1.2m (1–4ft)
✂ Cut back hard when flowers fade to induce a second flush
✿ Divide in early spring or late autumn

HAKONECHLOA

H. macra 'Aureola' is a fine, small grass, forming a low arching mound of gold leaves narrowly striped with green. They take on reddish tints later in the year, which often persist into winter. Best grown in reasonably moist, fertile soil. Lovely in containers.
○ ◑ H 25cm (10in), S 40cm (16in)
✂ Cut hard back in winter or spring
✿ Division in early spring

HEBE

As a general rule, the smaller-leaved hebes are much more dependable shrubs than their large-flowered cousins, which are not reliably hardy. They form neat, evergreen domes in all shades from pewter to deep green, some producing a good show of small flowers. The 'whipcord' hebes such

as bronze-yellow *H. ochracea* 'James Stirling' have small, scale-like leaves. All make attractive, easy ground-cover plants.
○ H 30–60cm (1–2ft), S 60cm–1m (2–3ft)
✂ Tidy wayward growth in spring
✿ Semi-ripe cuttings in late summer

HEDERA (Ivy) ☆

One of the toughest and most valuable of climbers: they are self-clinging, and provide evergreen cover in an enormous range of leaf colour and form. For ease of growth, choose a variety of the appropriate size for the allotted space, to avoid the need for cutting back. Gold-variegated forms such as *H. helix* 'Goldheart' colour best in sun. All ivies make useful groundcover in dry shade.
○ ◑ ● H 1–10m (3–30ft)
✂ None
✿ Semi-ripe cuttings, and cuttings in water in summer, layering in early spring

HOSTA (Plantain lily)

The most architectural of herbaceous perennials, forming wide rosettes of sculpted leaves. Colours range from green, through acid-yellow to some lovely glaucous shades, with any amount of variegated forms. White-rimmed *H.* 'Francee' is particularly attractive. Hostas make good groundcover, grow well on all but the driest soils, and make excellent container plants.
○ ◑ H 15cm–1.2m (6in–4ft), S 45cm–1.2m (18in–4ft)
✂ Cut back faded flowers in summer and trim off dead leaves in autumn
✿ Division in early spring

HYDRANGEA

Hydrangeas are valuable deciduous shrubs that provide long-lasting colour, the large, showy flowers appearing in summer and

Hakonechloa macra 'Aureola'

Hebe pinguifolia 'Pagei'

Lavandula angustifolia 'Hidcote'

gradually fading to red-tinted or buff through autumn and winter. The 'lacecap' forms of *H. macrophylla* such as 'Lanarth White' and 'Blue Wave' are particularly outstanding. Grow pink hydrangeas in alkaline soil, blue varieties in acid, peaty soil, or use the appropriate compost for container-grown plants. Best in a sheltered position. Leave faded flowers to protect new flower buds in spring.
○ ◑ H 1–2m (3–6ft), S 1–1.5m (3–5ft)
✄ No regular pruning required, but remove a few stems from congested plants in early spring if necessary
✺ Semi-ripe cuttings in midsummer

ILEX (Holly) ☆

These are indestructible evergreen shrubs or trees, good as background plants, specimens, or as tough, vandal-proof hedges. There are numerous variegated forms, which colour best in sun. Hollies can make prickly companions in smaller gardens, but there are many smooth-leaved forms, such as *I.* × *altaclerensis* 'Golden King'. Plant both male and female varieties for guaranteed berries.
○ ◑ H 1–20m (3–70ft), S 2–8m (6–25ft)
✄ Clip formal, shaped specimens as well as hedging hollies in mid-spring and midsummer
✺ Semi-ripe cuttings in late summer

IRIS

Irises are rhizomatous or bulbous perennials with a relatively short flowering period, but well worth growing for the beauty of the blooms, many of which bear delicate, complex markings. The range of colours is outstanding, particularly in the many rhizomatous varieties. There are small, spring-flowering irises for the rockery such as pale blue *I. reticulata* 'Cantab' and purple

I. r. 'J.S. Dijt', and late spring and summer varieties such as blue-flowered *I. pallida* 'Variegata', which will spread into large clumps, for pools and borders.
○ H 15cm–1.2m (6in–4ft)
✄ Cut back faded leaves of rhizomatous irises in late autumn
✺ Rhizomatous irises by division in late spring (*see p.51*), bulbous irises by division in early summer (*see p.61*)

JASMINUM (Jasmine)

Winter-flowering jasmine (*J. nudiflorum*) is a delightful shrub. It is easy to grow, very tolerant of shade, and produces beautiful star-shaped yellow flowers from mid-autumn to mid-spring. It is lovely left to tumble over a bank, and may also be supported against a wall. The more vigorous climbing summer jasmine (*J. officinale*), with its highly scented white flowers, needs a sunnier, sheltered position. Both are deciduous.
○ ◑ H and S winter jasmine 3m (10ft); summer jasmine 12m (40ft)
✄ Thin out old, flowered stems after flowering
✺ Semi-ripe cuttings in late summer, layering in early spring

JUNIPERUS (Juniper)

The juniper family contains many of the columnar conifers that provide stylish 'accents' in the formal garden, the rock garden and on the patio. Dwarf *J. communis* 'Compressa' and the taller *J. scopulorum* 'Skyrocket' are among the best. They are slow-growing, taking many years to reach their full height, and they grow well in any type of soil.
○ H 75cm–6m (30in–20ft), S 45–60cm (18in–2ft)
✄ None

✺ Cuttings of ripened wood in early autumn, in the same way as semi-ripe cuttings, but keep in cool conditions

LAVANDULA (Lavender)

With their long-lasting haze of flowers and delicious fragrance, lavenders are essential, easy-to-grow plants for any hot, sunny border. Dark purple *L. angustifolia* 'Hidcote' is exceptionally good, and ideal as a low informal hedge. The dwarf, white-flowered *L. a.* 'Nana Alba' is perfect for the rock garden.
○ H and S 30–60cm (1–2ft)
✄ Trim over in mid spring
✺ Semi-ripe cuttings in midsummer

LAVATERA (Mallow) ☆

The shrubby, perennial lavateras are spectacularly fast-growing, reaching 2m (6ft) in a single season. They are also very free-flowering, covered in trumpet-shaped blooms from summer to late autumn. Though not long-lived, they provide invaluable colour in beds and borders, and are easy to increase from cuttings. Pale pink, rosy-eyed *L.* 'Barnsley' is deservedly popular.
○ H and S 2m (6ft)
✄ Cut out any stems bearing flowers that are not true to type, and prune hard back in early spring
✺ Softwood cuttings in late spring

LILIUM (Lily)

Lilies are one of the most beautiful and desirable of summer plants, both for their exotic looks and for the rich perfumes that are especially strong on a warm evening. The waxy white trumpets of *L. regale*, backed with rosy purple are exceptionally well scented. Although most are perfectly hardy, it is easier to grow them in pots (*see p.111*) rather than the border, for better control of

Magnolia soulangeana

Mahonia x *media* 'Winter Sun'

Parthenocissus henryana

slugs, which can do a good deal of damage.
○ ◐ H 40cm–1.5m (16in–5ft)
✄ Remove faded flowers. Cut back dead
stems in late autumn
❧ No easy method

LONICERA (Honeysuckle)
With their sweet scent and showy flowers,
honeysuckles are invaluable twining climbers
for walls and pergolas. Evergreen, white-
flowered *L. japonica* 'Halliana' has the
longest flowering period, from spring to
late summer, while deciduous red-streaked
L. periclymenum 'Belgica' and 'Serotina' are
two of the most colourful.
○ ◐ H 4–10m (12–30ft)
✄ Thin out some of the older wood after
flowering. Hard prune neglected plants in
early spring (*see p.20*)
❧ Layering in early spring, hardwood
cuttings in late autumn

MAGNOLIA
M. x *soulangeana* is one of the loveliest of
a beautiful family of mainly deciduous trees
and shrubs, with large, goblet-shaped spring
flowers in a range of colours from white
and pearly-pink to rose-purple. The more
compact *M. stellata*, with its starry white
flowers in early to mid-spring, is an ideal
shrub for smaller gardens. Magnolias thrive
in any good, humus-rich soil (not chalk) in
a site sheltered from north and east winds.
All magnolias are very slow-growing.
○ ◐ H 3–6m (10–20ft), S 3–4m (10–12ft)
✄ Tidy wayward growth in spring
❧ Semi-ripe cuttings in late summer,
layering in early spring

MAHONIA (Oregon grape)
Mahonias are tough, stately evergreen
shrubs, with tiered sprays of shiny, holly-

like leaves. A useful background plant in
summer, mahonias come into their own
in winter, the tips of the branches bearing
great plumes of golden flowers from mid-
autumn to late winter. *M.* x *media* 'Winter
Sun' is a particularly fine plant, with bright
yellow flowers on arching shoots. There are
also smooth-leaved and globe-flowered
forms, but these do not have the same
impact. Grow in fairly fertile, humus-rich,
moist but well-drained soil.
○ ◐ ● H 2–4m (6–12ft), S 1–4m (3–12ft)
✄ Tidy wayward growth in spring
❧ Semi-ripe cuttings in late summer

MALUS (Crab apple) ☆
Crab apples are ideal ornamental trees for
small gardens. Reliable and undemanding,
they produce a flurry of white, pink or
crimson blossom in spring, followed by good
crops of small shiny fruit, which can persist
into winter. The rich yellow fruits of 'Golden
Hornet' are especially striking, while 'John
Downie' bears the best fruit for preserves.
'Royalty' is a good purple-leaved form.
○ H and S 4–8m (12–25ft)
✄ None
❧ Seed sown outdoors in autumn (seed of
named hybrids does not come true to type)

NARCISSUS (Daffodil)
No other spring flower is quite so welcome
as the daffodil. These bulbs are remarkably
versatile, with varieties suitable for beds,
borders, pots, tubs and even hanging
baskets. The smaller and species varieties are
normally called 'narcissi', the larger hybrids
'daffodils'. A combination of early, mid- and
late flowering varieties will provide flowers
from late winter right through to late spring.
N. 'February Gold', for example, is
exceptionally early, while the beautifully

scented white *N. poeticus* can still be flowering
in early summer.
○ ◐ H 10–50cm (4–20in)
✄ Nip off faded flower heads and cut back
dying leaves in mid-spring
❧ Division in early summer

PAEONIA (Peony)
The flowering period of peonies (late spring
and early summer) is relatively short, but
glorious, and they are well worth growing
in even the smallest garden. The ruffled
double varieties such as pink 'Bowl of
Beauty' and crimson 'Félix Crousse' are
the most striking, and many are deliciously
scented. The cut-leaved foliage is attractive
too, taking on reddish autumn tints. Grow
in good, fertile soil, and support the heavy
flowers by staking. Site where they can grow
on undisturbed – it is possible to lift and
divide them, but they may not flower again
for several years.
○ H and S 75cm–1m (30in–3ft)
✄ Remove stems of faded flowers
❧ Division in early spring or late autumn

PARTHENOCISSUS
(Virginia creeper) ☆
These vigorous, self-clinging climbers are
tremendously useful for covering large
expanses of wall. The autumn colour is
spectacular, ranging through red, bronze
and purple. Apple-green *P. henryana*
(Chinese Virginia creeper) is particularly
striking, the white-veined leaves turning
bright red in autumn. Good soil preparation
is vital when planting.
○ ◐ H 10–20m (30–70ft)
✄ Remove unwanted growth in summer
or early winter
❧ Softwood cuttings in early summer,
or winter

Philadelphus 'Belle Etoile'

Phlox paniculata 'Mother of Pearl'

Pulmonaria rubra 'Redstart'

❧ Softwood cuttings in early summer, hardwood cuttings in late autumn, layering in spring

PHILADELPHUS (Mock orange)

Deservedly popular, philadelphus is a tough, undemanding shrub, ideal for shady spots. It produces a mass of fragrant white flowers on arching stems in spring and early summer, and the single varieties are particularly graceful – *P*. 'Belle Etoile', for example, with a pale purple blotch at the base of each petal.

○ ◑ H and S 1–3m (3–10ft)

✂ Cut back flowered shoots and remove a few older stems if overcrowded in summer

❧ Softwood cuttings in late spring or early summer, hardwood cuttings in late autumn

PHLOX

P. paniculata is a colourful, dependable border perennial, and will increase into a sizable clump. Large heads of flowers are produced from midsummer to early autumn, in a range of colours to suit every planting scheme. Compact, pink-tinged 'Mother of Pearl' is especially attractive. If planted in a dry soil, it will need regular watering in hot weather to prevent the flowers from drooping.

○ H 75–90cm (30–36in), S 60–90cm (2–3ft)

✂ Dead-head to extend flowering, and cut to the ground in late autumn

❧ Division in early spring or late autumn

PRUNUS (Ornamental cherry)

P. serrula is a delightful small tree, with a neatly domed habit and year-round value from its silky, shining chestnut bark. *P. cerasifera* 'Nigra' (syn. *P.c.* 'Pissardii Nigra') provides a good show of pink flowers in spring, followed by dramatically dark purple

leaves, which are especially lovely when underplanted with golden-leaved shrubs. Both are deciduous.

○ H and S 10m (30ft)

✂ Remove any suckers that appear at the base of the trunk.

❧ Semi-ripe cuttings in midsummer

PULMONARIA (Lungwort)

Despite the uninviting name, these are very attractive and easy herbaceous perennials, with two seasons of interest. Cowslip-like heads of red, pink, blue or white flowers are produced in profusion in early spring. When these die back, dense rosettes of leaves appear, many varieties with attractive pale green or white marblings and spottings. Coral red *P. ubra*. 'Redstart' is one of the very earliest and can be in flower in midwinter. They form large clumps, and self-seed fairly freely.

○ ◑ H 30cm (1ft), S 45cm (18in)

✂ None

❧ Divide after flowering or in late autumn

PYRACANTHA (Firethorn)

Easy, evergreen shrubs, pyracanthas are especially valued for their mass of long-lasting red, orange or yellow berries. 'Orange Glow' is one of the most free-berrying of all. Pyracanthas look handsome trained against a wall, or around a doorway, but they are also useful as an impenetrable informal hedge. If training, wear stout gloves as protection against the fearsome thorns. A fertile, well-drained soil and sheltered site are essential.

○ ◑ H 2–3m (6–10ft), S 2–4m (6–12ft)

✂ Prune back wall-trained plants in early summer or midsummer. Remove wayward growths from free-standing plants in midsummer

❧ Semi-ripe cuttings in summer

RHODODENDRON (Rhododendrons and azaleas)

Because their flowering period (mid- to late spring) is relatively short, it is the evergreen rhododendrons and azaleas that give the best value, providing good strong foliage colour in winter. Many are dwarf, such as the popular 'Vuyk's Scarlet'. They are immensely showy when in flower, and the best effects can often be achieved by planting them singly rather than in groups, especially in dappled shade. All rhododendrons and azaleas require an acid soil.

○ ◑ H and S 1–3m (3–10ft)

✂ None

❧ Semi–ripe cuttings in late summer, layering in early spring

RIBES (Flowering currant)

R. sanguineum is a dependable, easy shrub for spring colour, producing dangling clusters of fuchsia-like flowers. Rich red 'Pulborough Scarlet' and pure white 'Tydeman's White' are especially good. 'Brocklebankii' has bright gold young foliage, fading to paler gold in summer.

○ H 1.2–3m (4–10ft), S 1.2–2.5m (4–8ft)

✂ Remove flowered shoots and a few older stems in late spring

❧ Hardwood cuttings in late autumn

ROBINIA (False acacia) ☆

The deciduous *R. pseudoacacia* 'Frisia' is one of the most delightful of small trees, a billowing froth of acacia-like leaves that are bright gold in spring, ageing to a fresh yellow-green. Its colour, and its graceful habit, make it an ideal specimen tree. It grows well in any soil, but should be planted in a sheltered position so that wind does not snap the brittle branches.

○ H 10m (30ft), S 6m (20ft)

Sedum spectabile

Sorbus vilmorinii

Thymus serphyllum 'Pink Chintz'

✄ No regular pruning, but any branch removal should be done in late summer to prevent the loss of sap

✿ Green-leaved *R. pseudoacacia* from seed sown in autumn

ROSA (Rose)

In all their wonderful diversity, there are roses to suit all garden situations – from climbers and ramblers for walls and pergolas, to charming ground-cover roses to clothe an awkward slope with style. There are also any number of charming miniatures that will grow happily in pots on the patio. Try, where possible, to choose disease-resistant varieties. Require fertile, well-drained soil preferably in an open site.

○ H and S: climbers and ramblers H 3–10m (10–30ft), S 2–6m (6–20ft); bush roses H 30cm–2.2m (12in–7ft), S 30cm–1ft (12in–3ft); shrub roses H 1–2m (3–6ft), S 60cm–2m (2–6ft)

✄ Climbers *see p.93*, ramblers *see p.75*, all other roses *see p.19*

✿ Hardwood cuttings cuttings in late autumn. Large-flowered (hybrid tea) and cluster-flowered (floribunda) roses can be difficult to propagate

SALIX (Willow) ☆

The willow family encompasses mighty deciduous trees to neat shrubs, in a wide range of forms. In larger gardens, the twisted willow, *S. babylonica* var. *pekinensis* 'Tortuosa', makes a splendid specimen, each branch, twig and leaf being sinuously curved. The stiffly weeping Kilmarnock willow (*S. caprea* 'Kilmarnock') and silver-leaved coyote willow (*S. exigua*) are fine plants for smaller spaces. Require deep, moist but well-drained soil and dislike chalk.

○ H and S 2–15m (6–50ft)

✄ Remove wayward growths of Kilmarnock willow in late winter to maintain a neatly weeping shape

✿ Hardwood cuttings late autumn, and cuttings in water in midsummer

SAMBUCUS (Elder)

The common wayside elder, *S. nigra*, is a charming deciduous tree, and there are many fine, easily grown garden hybrids derived from this and other species. The leaves of *S. nigra* 'Guincho Purple' are a deep black-purple, providing a lovely contrast to the pink-tinged flower heads. *S. racemosa* 'Sutherland Gold' is a fine cut-leaved gold for sun, while the similar *S. r.* 'Plumosa Aurea' prefers shade.

○ ◐ H and S 2.5–5m (8–15ft)

✄ Hard prune golden varieties in late winter or early spring for larger, brighter leaves

✿ Hardwood cuttings in late autumn

SAXIFRAGA (Saxifrage)

The saxifrages are some of the easiest of rock garden plants, and a single small plant will soon increase into a sizeable clump. The variety of leaf colour and form is astonishing, from feathery golds to succulent-leaved silvers; many also have highly attractive flowers, such as pretty pink *S. × irvingii* 'Jenkinsiae'. Sharply drained conditions are essential. Good grown in pots.

○ ◐ H (in flower) 5–45cm (2–18in), S 10–30cm (4in–1ft)

✄ Trim off faded flowers

✿ Detach non-flowering rosettes in late spring, remove lower leaves and place in pots of well-drained compost to grow on

SEDUM (Stonecrop)

Easy, clump-forming succulent-leaved plants for borders and rock gardens. Cultivars of

S. spectabile (ice plant) are ideal for a sunny border, with showy flower heads in autumn. Alpine sedums are very diverse in colour and form, and the only one to avoid is *S. acre* (biting stonecrop), which can be very invasive. All sedums must have good drainage.

○ H (in flower) 5–45cm (2–18in), S 15–60cm (6in–2ft)

✄ Trim off faded flowers

✿ Division in early spring

SOLANUM

S. crispum is a vigorous and exceptionally free-flowering scarmbling climber. The large sprays of yellow-eyed blue flowers are produced from early summer through to early autumn. It is evergreen, but may drop its leaves in a very cold winter.

○ H 5–6m (15–20ft)

✄ Prune out any damaged, wayward or over-long stems in early to mid-spring

✿ Semi-ripe cuttings in summer

SORBUS (Mountain ash, rowan) ☆

Rowans are robust, easy deciduous trees for all gardens, and are immensely attractive. The white spring blossom produces heavy crops of red, white or yellow berries, the white and yellow persisting well into winter, while red berries will feed the birds. The ferny leaves colour up beautifully in autumn. *S. vilmorinii*, at only 5m (15ft) tall, will fit into even the smallest garden.

○ ◐ H 5–10m (15–30ft), S 5–8m (15–25ft)

✄ None

✿ Semi-ripe cuttings in midsummer

SPIRAEA

Summer-flowering *S. japonica* is a good, undemanding deciduous shrub for a sunny border, bearing heads of pink or white flowers

Tulipa kaufmanniana

Vitis vinifera 'Purpurea'

Weigela 'Florida Variegata'

over a long period. Those with coloured foliage are particularly attractive; compact *S. j.* 'Golden Princess' retains its bright gold colour right through summer. Flowers best on reasonably moist, fertile soil.
○ H 45cm–1.5m (18in–5ft), S 60cm–1.5m (2–5ft)
✂ Thin out and cut back in early spring
✎ Semi-ripe cuttings in summer

TAXUS (Yew) ☆

T. baccata (common yew) is one of the loveliest of hedging conifers – densely clothed with evergreen foliage, and a rich, deep green. For the garden, *T. b.* 'Fastigiata' (Irish yew) makes a dark, dramatic 'accent' plant, forming a tall column topped with several spires. All yews are slow-growing, tough and undemanding; they grow happily in chalk or acid soils, and tolerate exposed or polluted sites in full sun or dense shade. The berries are poisonous.
○ ◑ ● H 6m (20ft), S 2–8m (6–25ft) unclipped
✂ Clip hedges as needed. Overgrown hedges can be renovated in spring
✎ *T. baccata* from seed, named varieties from semi-ripe cuttings in late summer

THYMUS (Thyme)

In addition to its culinary uses, thyme is a good, easy plant for any well-drained soil, forming neat cushions of tiny aromatic leaves. Foliage colours vary from green to gold, silver and grey. Golden *T.* × *citriodorus* 'Aureus', silver-variegated *T. vulgaris* 'Silver Posie' and grey-green *T. serpyllum* 'Pink Chintz' are especially attractive. The pink, purple or white flowers are a good pollen source for bees. Not all are suitable for culinary use, but two of the best are *T. vulgaris* and *T.* × *citriodorus* (lemon

thyme), together with their cultivars. Good for planting in paving, and excellent in pots.
○ H (in flower) 10–30cm (4in–1ft), S 15–45cm (6–18in)
✂ Trim over after flowering
✎ Division in spring

TULIPA (Tulip)

Tulips are invaluable spring bulbs, providing a succession of flowers right through spring, in an incredible diversity of colour and form. The small waterlily tulips of the Kaufmanniana group are among the earliest, and are excellent grown in pots and window boxes. For beds and borders, there is a whole array of taller tulips, from formally upright single varieties such as deep maroon 'Queen of Night' to luscious doubles like pink 'Angélique'. They need to be planted 15cm (6in) deep in order to establish well. Tulips prefer a fertile, well-drained soil with protection from strong winds.
○ H 10–60cm (4in–2ft)
✂ Remove faded flowers and cut back dead foliage
✎ Division in early summer

VIBURNUM ☆

The viburnum family of shrubs contains many easily grown plants of outstanding merit. Excellent choices for winter colour and scent are the attractive pink-flowered, deciduous *V.* × *bodnantense* 'Dawn' and the white-flowered evergreen *V. tinus* 'Eve Price' – both flower over a very long period in winter and into early spring. A good choice for late spring and summer is *V. sargentii* 'Onondaga', with bronzy young foliage and myriad dusky pink 'lacecap' flowers.
○ ◑ H 2.5–3m (8–10ft), S 2–3m (6–10ft)
✂ Tidy wayward growth in spring
✎ Semi-ripe cuttings in summer

VITIS (Grape vine)

There are numerous highly ornamental vines. If you have the space, the vigorous *V. coignetiae* is a particularly wonderful climber, the huge heart-shaped leaves turning fiery red in autumn. *V. vinifera* 'Purpurea' is more restrained, and the lobed leaves are claret-coloured in summer, turning to deep purple shades in autumn.
○ ◑ H 6–15m (20–50ft)
✂ Cut back in early winter if necessary
✎ Layering in early spring

WEIGELA

A good, undemanding deciduous shrub for late spring and early summer, producing foxglove-like flowers in all shades from white to deep red. The most useful weigelas are the white-variegated forms such as *W. praecox* 'Variegata' and *W.* 'Florida Variegata' which provide additional summer interest.
○ ◑ H 2.5m (8ft), S 2–2.5m (6–8ft)
✂ After flowering, thin out older stems and flowered shoots
✎ Semi-ripe cuttings in summer, hardwood cuttings in autumn

WISTERIA

The cascading white, pink or violet blossom of wisteria is one of the most spectacular sights of late spring and early summer. Careful training and twice-yearly pruning is essential for maximum flowers. *W. sinensis* (Chinese wisteria) is a vigorous plant, *W. floribunda* (Japanese wisteria) rather neater. The flowers of *W. f.* 'Macrobotrys' can be 90cm–1.2m (3–4ft) long. Grow in a sheltered south- or west-facing position.
○ ◑ H 8–20m (25–70ft)
✂ Shorten sideshoots in late summer and late winter (*see pp. 74 and 117*)
✎ Layering in spring

Glossary

Acid soil Soil with a pH of less than 7, which is essential for plants such as rhododendrons. A simple soil test kit will determine the acidity of your soil.

Aerate To loosen and let air into the soil, e.g. by spiking the lawn.

Alkaline soil Soil with a pH of more than 7, determined as for acid soil. Chalk soils have high alkalinity.

Alpine A term often used loosely to describe any plant that is suitable for growing in the rock garden.

Annual A plant that germinates, flowers, sets seed and dies in a single growing season.

Aquatic plant Any plant that grows in water, whether it is submerged, floating, or has its roots underwater and its top-growth on, or above, the surface of the water.

Bare-root Deciduous woody plants and fruit that are dug up when dormant in autumn and early winter and supplied with the roots bare of soil.

Bedding plants Annuals, biennials and tender perennials that are planted out temporarily.

Biennial A plant that produces leaves in its first year, flowers in its second year, then dies.

Biological control A non-chemical way to control pests, using commercially supplied predators.

Bud The point on a stem from which new growth emerges.

Bulb Underground storage organ consisting of fleshy scales.

Canopy The extent of cover provided by the leaves and branches of trees and shrubs.

Capillary matting A synthetic material that draws up water by capillary action.

Catch crop A fast-maturing crop interplanted between slow-growing crops to maximize the use of ground.

Cloche A portable glass, plastic or polycarbonate cover used to protect crops against frosts and to warm the soil before planting or sowing.

Collar The part of a plant where the top-growth emerges.

Corm A bulbous underground stem, e.g. crocus.

Crocks Broken pieces of clay pot, placed curved side up in the base of terracotta pots for good drainage.

Crown In a tree, the framework of branches. In a herbaceous plant, the point at which new growth emerges in spring.

Cuttings Portions of plant that are potted up to form new plants.

Dead-heading Removing faded flowers to prevent a plant from setting seed.

Deciduous Any plant that sheds its leaves in autumn.

Die-back Any shoot that begins to die back from the tip.

Division Propagating clump-forming plants by dividing them up.

Dormancy A resting period when a plant displays no signs of growth.

Drill A furrow in the soil into which seeds are sown.

Ericaceous Of compost with a high acid content; of plants, such as those of the *Erica* family, that require an acid soil or compost.

Framework The main, permanent branches of a tree or shrub, or of a climber such as wisteria.

Fungicide Proprietary chemical that kills fungi such as powdery mildew.

Germination The point at which a seed starts to grow.

Grafting A method of propagation involving the joining together of two plants. Most roses, for example, are grafted onto vigorous wild rose rootstocks, while many weeping standard trees are grafted onto the roots and stems of another, related variety.

Groundcover Any plant that produces a dense leaf cover that suppresses weeds.

Growing point The point from which most growth is made – i.e. the tips of main stems and side branches or stems.

Half hardy A plant that will tolerate a few degrees of frost but will be killed by hard frosts.

Hardy A plant that will survive indefinitely in the open garden, whatever the weather.

Herbaceous A non-woody plant that dies back to the crown in winter.

Horticultural fleece A light, opaque fleecy material that protects plants from frost and insect pests.

Insecticide Any proprietary chemical or organic pesticide that kills insect pests without harming plants.

Layering A propagation method for woody plants, which encourages a shoot to root while still attached to the parent plant. The commonest method is to pin the shoot to the ground and then cover it with soil.

Landscape fabric A woven polypropylene material which suppresses weeds completely when laid out on the soil, but allows rain to penetrate.

Leader The main stem of a plant – usually applied to the central, tallest stem of a tree.

Loam Soil with a good balance of sand, clay and organic matter. Loam-based compost is a proprietary mix.

Marginal A plant that grows in shallow water at the edge of a pond or a pool.

Mulch Material such as bark chips, cocoa shell, gravel and polythene, laid on the soil to conserve moisture and suppress weeds. Organic mulches also provide nutrients and improve the soil structure.

Naturalizing
Growing plants so that they look as if they are in the wild, e.g. daffodils (*Narcissus*) in grass.

Offset A young plant that forms at the base of the parent plant, e.g. small bulbs that form around the parent bulb and gradually separate out to form separate plants.

Organic matter A wide range of natural materials, including home-made compost and well-rotted manure, which can be used as a mulch or for digging in to improve soil condition.

Overwinter To give winter protection to a tender plant that can then be planted outdoors the following summer, e.g. geranium (*Pelargonium*).

Oxygenator A pond plant that is submerged and releases oxygen into the water.

Peat Moisture-retentive, acid soil derived from peat bogs. Many composts are peat-based, but peat-substitutes, which are more environmentally friendly, are now more widely available.

Perennial Any plant that will live for at least three seasons, although most will far exceed this.

Pesticide Any proprietary substance that kills insect pests and mites.

pH A scale measuring the relative acidity or alkalinity of soil which helps to determine the range of plants that can be grown in that soil.

Pinch out To remove the growing tip of the main stem of a plant, to encourage a branching habit. Can also be used on side stems, to promote bushiness.

Pollination The transfer of pollen from a male to a female flower in order for it to fruit or set seed.

Potting on Transferring a plant to a larger pot.

Pricking out Transferring seedlings from the original pot or seedtray to a larger pot or seedtray.

Propagation Increasing plants by several methods, including seed, bulbs, cuttings, division and layering.

Propagator A heated or unheated box with a clear lid, used for raising seedlings and cuttings.

Rhizomatous A creeping, woody stem, normally close to the soil surface, that stores energy and produces leaves and roots along its length, e.g. rhizomatous irises.

Rootstock The root system of a plant grafted onto the top-growth of another. Many roses are grafted onto wild rose rootstocks to create a more vigorous root system.

Runner A stem which runs along the ground and roots at one or more points to form new plants, e.g. strawberries.

Scarify The removal of moss or thatch from the surface of the lawn, using a rake or scarifier.

Self-seed The shedding of seeds that form seedlings near a parent plant, with no help from the gardener.

Slow-release fertilizer A fertilizer that releases its nutrients over a long period of time.

Specimen plant A particularly striking plant that is used as the centrepiece of a planting, or in a prominent position where it can be viewed from all sides.

Spent Of flowers – dead or dying; of mushroom compost – formerly used for mushroom production.

Spur A short branch that bears flowers. Normally used in relation to fruit trees.

Standard A tree with at least 2m (6ft) of clear stem below the branches, or a shrub that has been trained on a single clear stem.

Subsoil The soil beneath topsoil, generally denser and less fertile.

Sucker Growth arising from the rootstock of a grafted plant. Also any growth produced from below ground on a plant on its own roots.

Systemic Any pesticide or fungicide that is absorbed into a plant's system, giving longer-lasting protection than 'contact' killers.

Thatch A layer of dead organic matter (generally grass clippings) that accumulates on the soil surface of lawns.

Tender Any plant that will be killed by frost.

Thinning Removing surplus plant material, e.g. overcrowded seedlings, or congested growth on trees and shrubs.

Top-dress To renew the top level of compost in a container; to apply organic or inorganic matter to a lawn to feed and improve its texture; or to apply fertilizers, mulches, or stone or grit around plants

Topsoil The upper, usually fertile, layer of soil.

Transpiration The loss of water by evaporation from the surface of leaves and stems.

Trench A strip of deeply dug soil.

Tuber A swollen storage organ, usually underground, e.g. potato.

Vermiculite Material used for covering seedlings and to aid water retention when added to compost.

Water-retaining crystals Sugar-like crystals that swell into a frogspawn gel. When mixed with compost, they act as mini-reservoirs, helping to conserve moisture.

Waterlogged Soil that is saturated and drains very slowly.

Woody plant A shrub or tree with fibrous stems that persist above ground level all year round.

Index

bulbs, dividing spring 61
cuttings, propagation by 69
dead-heading 58, 61, 62, 64, 67, 77
feeding 65
fence and wall maintenance 76
holiday care 77
mulching 62, 65
ponds 67
pruning 59, 72, 74, 75
strawberries, planting 79
vegetables 63, 78
watering 60, 65, 70, 71, 77

T

tomatoes, planting in growbags 63
tools and equipment, maintenance 121
top-dressing
    containers, plants in 34
    lawns 28
    rock gardens 16, 94
trees 105
    branches, pruning 120
    climbers on 92
    containers, growing in 34, 62, 112
    fruit, pruning 72, 123
    planting 101
    suckers 68

transplanting 91
weeping standard, pruning 120

V

vegetables 89
    frost, protection from 44
    ground preparation 107
    growbags 63
    maximizing crop 78
    mulching 78
    pests, protection from 72, 89
    raised beds 41, 43, 113
    seed, growing from 26, 29, 78
    watering 60, 70, 78, 89
vine weevils 126

W

walls
    alpines 16
    climbers 15, 65
    maintenance 76
    wall shrubs 15, 65
watering 60, 65
    alpines in walls and crevices 16
    automatic systems 53, 62, 70, 77
    autumn 83
    capillary 77

conserving water 60
containers and window boxes 52, 62, 70, 77, 83
flower towers and pouches 54
growbags 63
hanging baskets 53, 62
holiday care 77
lawns 71
vegetables 60, 70, 78, 89
weeds 82, 129–31
    lawns 35, 36, 37, 55, 131
    mulching 17, 65
    paved areas 25, 103
wheelbarrows, maintenance 121
wildlife, caring for 104
wind, protection from 30, 32, 90, 100
window boxes 24, 52, 77, 98
winter
    clear-up 121
    planting hedges 118
    pruning 116, 117, 119, 120, 123
    training hedges 119
wisteria
    propagation 22, 51
    training and pruning 66, 74, 117
wooden tubs, maintenance 121
worm casts, on lawns 35

Acknowledgments

The publishers would like to thank the following organizations and individuals for their kind permission to reproduce the photographs in this book:

Jonathan Buckley 56–57, 73; Frank Lane Picture Agency/Ray Bird 72; Garden Picture Library/John Baker 113, /Jon Bouchier 86, /Mark Bolton 138 left, /Linda Burgess 6, 92, /Brian Carter 26, /Erika Craddock 100 top right, /Ron Evans 100 bottom, 118, /Vaughan Fleming 126, /Christopher Gallagher 40, /John Glover 21, 35, 65, 109, 116 top right, 116 bottom right, 123, 139 left, /John Glover/The Anchorage, Kent 37, /Sunniva Harte 31, 58, /Michael Howes 96, 107, /Neil Holmes 80–81, 82, 103 bottom right, 128 bottom right, 136 centre, /Jacqui Hurst 43, /Roger Hyam 16, /Lamontagne

117 top right, /Jane Legate 39, /Mayer/Le Scanff 12–13, 41, 44 bottom, 49 top left, 50, 86, 90 bottom right, /Clive Nichols/Coates Manor Garden, Sussex 134 left, /Howard Rice 114–115, /Gary Rogers 131, /J S Sira 2, /Frederick Strauss 77, /Brigitte Thomas 28, /Juliette Wade 63, 110, /Mel Watson 79, 97, /Didier Willery 75,/Steven Wooster 55, 95, 106; John Glover 1, 45, 48, 54, 66, 90 top right, 139 centre; Holt Studios International/ Nigel Cattlin 101; Anne Hyde 4–5, 70, 105, 119; Andrew Lawson Photography 23, 32, 52, 53, 62, 64 bottom right, 68, 71, 87, 133 right, 135 right, 135 centre, 136 right, 137 right, 138 right, /designer: Jonathan Baillie 76, /Rofford Manor 122; Octopus Publishing Group Ltd/Sue Atkinson 94, /Paul Barker 130, /Jerry Harpur 139 right,

/Stephen Robson 74 top, /Stephen Robson/ Sooke Harbour House 42; NHPA/Stephen Dalton 104; Clive Nichols Garden Pictures 14, 17, 20, 74 bottom right, 88, 98, 99, 102, 111, /Cecil & Yvonne Bicknell 59, /designer: C. Cordy 112, /Mr Fraser/ J Treyer-Evans 67, /The Old School House, Essex 25, /Graham Strong 85; Photos Horticultural 1, 15, 18, 19, 22, 24, 29, 30, 46, 47, 60, 61, 64 top right, 69, 78, 84, 89, 120, 121, 124, 127, 129, 132, 133 left, 133 centre, 134 centre, 134 right, 135 left, 136 left, 137 left, 137 centre, 138 centre; Derek St Romaine 93; Harry Smith Collection 108; Jo Whitworth 33.

The publishers also wish to thanks Polly Boyd for her editorial help.